LIFE'S LITTLE LAUGHS

DELIGHTFUL TALES FROM OUR AWHO SOCIETY

SK KATARIA

Life's Little Laughs : Delightful Tales From Our AWHO Society, is dedicated to my beloved father **Late Sh CL Kataria**, an extraordinary educationalist who not only shaped minds but also defined true handsomeness - both in spirit and form. His brilliance, compassion, and strength of character continue to inspire and guide me everyday. Though he may have departed, his presence and influence remain an eternal part of my journey.

In loving memory, always.

Contents

Contents

Contents

Preface

In Life's Little Laughs : Delightful Stories From Our AWHO Society, a senior Army veteran with 35 years of experience in combat engineering and infrastructure development takes a whimsical turn towards lighter side of life. Known for his sharp wit, the author moves seamlessly from military literature to everday society issues, crafting a collection of amusing and insightful stories.

Set in a bustling residential AWHO Society in Sector 114, Mohali, each story is drawn from real-life encounters, highlighting the quirks, interactions, and mishaps of community living. The author, a golf enthusiast, amateur singer, and passionate traveler, brings his zest for life into his tales, offering a humorous yet heartfelt exploration of human connections.

L3 isn't just light-hearted anecdotes; it's a reminder of the importance of unity, patience and understanding within a community. With its engaging narrative style and meaningful takeaways, this book offers something for everyone - a quick chuckle or a moment of reflection. Prepare to be entertained, amused, and inspired.

Brigadier SK Kataria (Retd)
kataria236@yahoo.com
October 2024

Acknowledgements

This book would have not been possible without the unwavering support of my wife, **Sapna Kataria**. From the very beginning - conceiving the theme, shaping the narrative, and most importantly selecting the punchlines that are the soul of these short stories - she has been by my side every step of the way. Sapna dedicated countless hours, patiently listening to my drafts and offering suggestions to improve them. She played a crucial role in arranging the stories in a way that maintained interest until the very end. As a matter of fact, our evening walks became the breeding ground for many of the ideas, where the core structure of the stories was formed. I am immensely grateful to her for her love, patience and the contribution to this project.

I would also like to thank my friend **Mr SS Giani**, who lives in the same tower as I do in our AWHO Society in Sector 114, Mohali. After reading my first story on our Society Whatsapp Group, he was highly impressed with my writing and encouraged me to explore writing blogs. His words gave me the push I perhaps needed to further develop my ideas. However, as the stories unfolded, I realised that a book was the best format to present this collection. Thank you Mr Giani, for your motivation and belief in my work, which helped guide me to this point.

CHAPTER ONE

THE JOURNEY OF THE ACCIDENTAL STORYTELLER

I've always had this itch to write, something I just couldn't ignore. If it wasn't golf or music, then it had to be words that kept me entertained. It all began innocently enough from my rare light-hearted posts on our Society WhatsApp Group. A witty phrase here, a quirky idiom there, responding to random questions or odd remarks. Surprisingly, those little messages started gaining attention; people loved them.

It escalated quickly. Soon, I found myself drafting important RWA instructions, advisory on society rules, and responses to the ever-buzzing issues. No one asked me to do this, but I felt compelled to contribute.

But as my posts grew in frequency and length, I noticed something strange. Some residents began to refer to me as the official RWA spokesperson. It wasn't the title I was after or would like it either. One day, as I typed out yet another formal post, my daughter, fresh off her MBA from Greater Noida, peeked over my shoulder.

"Dad, why do you sound so stiff?" she asked, frowning at my screen. "You could make these messages more engaging."

"What do you mean, engaging? These are official announcements!" I replied, a bit defensive.

She shrugged, "Just think about it."

That night, her words kept me awake till quite late. What if I could convey these instructions as short stories - something enjoyable, something that would connect with the residents? The next morning, I was ready to try.

A resident had sent me a lengthy chain of messages detailing a disagreement he'd had with the RWA, full of emotion and frustration. I saw it as a perfect opportunity to craft a narrative. I transformed his situation into a light-hearted tale about navigating the labyrinth of community discipline. I posted it in the group, uncertain of how it would be received.

To my surprise, the story resonated. The complaint subsided, but the reactions were underwhelming - just a few likes.

Instead of feeling defeated, I took it as a challenge. Each day, I began turning mundane society issues into engaging narratives. Golf outings became hilarious episodes, maintenance issues were recast as adventures, and even parking disputes turned into comical sagas. I was getting faster at it, too; what once took me upto six hours now took just three.

One day, one friend from our Society called and said, "I enjoy your stories. Why don't you share them on a blog? People would love to read them." I laughed it off. "I'm not in this for fame; I just enjoy writing. I am too moody."

But the idea lingered. A week later, my friend sent me a PDF containing my story, published in a well-known newspaper. I was thrilled. My wife urged me to share it with our Society and Coursemates WhatsApp groups.

When I did, the response was overwhelming. My phone buzzed with congratulatory messages, and likes poured in from all sides. I was astonished. What had changed?

My wife smiled knowingly. "You remember that news bite that aired years ago on many national TV channels when you were the Chief Engineer? It's funny how people sometimes need that external validation to appreciate something they already enjoy," she said.

It wasn't just about the words anymore; it was about perception. I learnt that stories could connect us and make our everyday lives a little more colourful. Now, I write not for likes and thumbs ups but to share moments that might make someone smile or see things differently.

CHAPTER TWO

WHEN A GOLF DROUGHT TURNS YOU INTO THE RWA'S UNEXPECTED SAVIOUR

It's just a few days old story when my WhatsApp exploded with a flurry of frantic messages from a flat owner, complete with a clutter of attachments that seemed to have been circulated more times than a viral meme. He was at his wits' end with the RWA's radio silence and, seeing my barrage of Society updates (courtesy heavy rains that rendered SEPTA unplayable), decided I must be the unofficial RWA Guru.

His main beef was with the location and timing of the new STPs. Even though the details had been shared umpteen times, I took it upon myself to clarify. I assured him the STPs wouldn't sprout up right in front of any towers and that, after all the formalities, we should see them in action within two years.

His response? A swift thumbs-up and a "thanks" emoji. But then came the kicker - a cryptic "partly."

Now I'm left scratching my head. Was "partly" his way of saying I nailed it but missed the spot, or is this just a teaser for the next episode of our RWA saga? Guess I'll have to stay tuned for the sequel!

Trust he was simply sipping on something stronger while mulling over my answer?

CHAPTER THREE

A Game of Golf, a Shift in Perception

After a long 15-day break, the early morning routine resumed with a sense of urgency as we set off at 0530 hours for our beloved SEPTA Golf Course. "If we don't play golf in the week, life seems to grind to a halt," my friend had joked as we carpooled, catching up on everything from national news to our Society happenings during the overcast 40-minute ride.

We arrived 20 minutes ahead of our tee-off time, as usual, prepping caddies and squeezing in some warm-up swings. While the game is generally serious - especially with breakfast on the line for the loser - there is always room for the occasional laugh. Midway through, we took our 20-minute breakfast break, chatting about stock market trends, sipping tea, and mapping out strategies for the next nine holes.

The return journey, though longer, was pleasant enough, except my friend seemed unusually upset. He hadn't played his best game, but what really bothered him was his recent visa rejection, coupled with a dismissive comment from a friend about the distance to our Society. "It's too far at the end of Mohali," the friend had said, making my buddy feel even more down.

Sensing his mood, I threw out a spontaneous thought - "It's all about perception. Sure, from Panchkula, our Society is at the end of Mohali. But from Ropar, it's at the beginning!" That little shift in perspective brought a smile to his face, lightening the mood as we neared home. Five hours after we had left, our game concluded - not just on the course, but in how we saw the world around us.

CHAPTER FOUR

BUILDING TRUST, ONE ACT OF KINDNESS AT A TIME

Every morning and evening, I am greeted by the car cleaners in our Society - "Sat Sri Akaal" or "Namaste, Sir!" Their smiles, despite long workdays, lifts my spirits, and I always respond with warmth. But little did I know, behind those smiles lay untold stories of struggle and resilience.

When I fell ill once, one car cleaner even came to my home to check on me, while others expressed concern during my walks. I realized how deeply connected we had become over time, despite their own hardships. These small gestures of care spoke volumes about their empathy.

One day, I asked a cleaner how many cars he worked on daily. His answer surprised me - cycling for 20 minutes to clean 10 to 12 cars each in the morning and evening, working elsewhere during the day, all while barely managing to sustain his family of four. Poverty, he said, felt like a curse. I walked away, feeling both grateful for my own blessings and saddened by the weight of his words.

In another instance, a cleaner shared how many residents argued over car-cleaning fees or delayed payments. On top of that, his landlord threatened to evict him if he didn't pay rent on time. Life, he said, was simply passing by. His plight stayed with me, a reminder of how easily we overlook the challenges of those around us.

The situation took a deeper turn when I brought up the topic of thefts in our Society with one of the cleaners. His response was poignant - "Whenever something gets stolen, we're always the first ones people suspect. Do we look like thieves?" His words lingered, and I realized we were missing something crucial. These cleaners, who spent hours in our community, were actually an untapped resource for surveillance. If we trusted them more and involved them in monitoring suspicious activities, they could help us keep our Society safe.

Another evening, despite being in a bad mood due to some maintenance issue in my flat, a cleaner approached me with a request during my walk. They were hauling buckets of water from the ground floor to the basement to wash cars. "Could we arrange for water in the basement?" I told him to talk to the Estate Manager, but he explained that previous attempts had been shut down with warnings about forming a 'union.' It was disheartening.

Determined to help, I raised the issue at the next RWA meeting. The solution was simple - use the existing fire hydrants in the basement to supply water for car washing. This small change saved them an hour of labour each day and significantly reduced their fatigue. One cleaner later thanked me, saying how much easier his work had become.

But the real lesson came as I reflected on the entire experience. Trust had been the missing piece all along. When we start showing trust in the car cleaners - whether by addressing their needs or involving them in solutions like surveillance - it not only benefits them, but also the whole community. Trust begets trust. By supporting them, we can gain a valuable ally in keeping our Society safe. They are not just workers but part of the fabric of our community.

CHAPTER FIVE

FAME, FLASH, AND A LESSON IN HUMILITY

As we prepared to move into our new flat, my ever-faithful orderly, who had been with me for over a decade, diligently took charge of overseeing the renovation. His trips from Chandimandir to the Society became routine, with each visit ending in the same ritual - detailed updates, followed by an unmistakable frown.

"Why do you always look like you've been handed a punishment after these debriefs?" I asked, finally unable to ignore it.

He hesitated before blurting out, "Sir, I keep running into these folk singers and wannabe actors in the Society. They act like they own the place. I've tried asking for selfies, but they barely look at me."

I was amused but also perplexed. "That's it? That's what's making you sulk? Forget about them. Just focus on your work."

Months later, we moved into our new flat, our humble haven. Evening walks soon became part of our routine, and during one of these days, a yellow BMW zipped by us, a green Lamborghini on another day and a black Harley Davidson almost everyday. My wife, always observant, exclaimed, "These guys must be loaded!"

Curiosity piqued, we asked the security supervisor about these speed demons. "Sir, those are the Punjabi singers and budding actors. They don't follow the rules, don't slow down, and think they're some kind of royalty," he said, rolling his eyes.

This brought back my orderly's grumbles. And soon, our Society's WhatsApp Group became a stage for these so-called stars, flaunting their reels filmed in the balconies, and outside Mr Green, the local vegetable vendor. While our esteemed defence officers mingled humbly, the "celebrities" strutted around as if the world revolved around their two-seater sports cars.

The contrast became glaring. While the majority of the residents were - men of genuine accomplishment - were approachable and down-to-earth, these flashy newcomers with oversized gold chains had an air of unwarranted arrogance. The cherry on top came one day at the RWA office.

The security supervisor had just finished complaining about one of these celebrities when in sauntered a young man - stocky, decked out in nikkar and slippers, a gold chain so heavy it could probably secure a rifle in the kote. Without even a nod of acknowledgment, he slumped into a chair, completely unbothered by the audience before him.

"This security supervisor keeps pestering me about getting a Parkplus tag for my car," he began. "But I'm a celebrity, you see. It's a security risk for me to have one."

Before anyone could process his masterpiece of logic, the General Secretary, clearly unimpressed, fired back, "Your entry without a Parkplus tag is a bigger security risk for everyone else in the Society."

The young star was left speechless, his bravado disappearing as quickly as his reasoning. He slinked out, the issue seemingly resolved for good.

As I watched the spectacle unfold then, I can't help but think of the legend Ratan Tata now - a man who could buy a fleet of Lamborghinis just for the fun of it but chose not to. He didn't need a spotlight; he was the spotlight. In fact, he was the kind of man who, if you asked for a selfie, would probably take it himself and make sure you looked good in it.

And so, as I watched our gold-draped celebrity walk out, I couldn't help but smile. Some people drive fancy cars to be noticed. Others could walk unnoticed through a crowd and still leave the deepest impression.

CHAPTER SIX

THE GREAT CYLINDER CAPER : WEIGH BEFORE YOU PAY!

The doorbell rang and I rushed to answer it. There stood the LPG delivery boy, a bulky cylinder by his side. "Did you order one?" I called out to my wife. "Yes!" she confirmed. I was puzzled. We were only two people in our flat, and we had just gotten a new cylinder a couple of days ago. How could it be finished already?

"Are you sure we needed a new one so soon?" I asked politely. Before my wife could answer, the delivery boy interjected, holding up his vintage weighing machine with a practiced smile. *"Sardi bahut hai, isliye gas jaldi khatam hoti hai!"* ("It's very cold these days, that's why the gas finishes quickly!").

I raised an eyebrow, not entirely convinced, but there wasn't much I could do. He weighed the cylinder quickly, and I, preoccupied, just paid and let him go.

The doubt, however, lingered. I couldn't quite shake off the feeling that something wasn't adding up. So, next time we were at the market, my wife and I bought a shiny digital weighing machine. We even tested it at the shop, measuring everything in sight, making sure it was as accurate as it could be.

Soon enough, the gas was running out again - this time, in just over two weeks. My wife ordered a new cylinder, and right on time, the Indane lorry rolled in with its load of gas cylinders. The same delivery boy came up, lugging the new cylinder, and rang our bell. I stepped outside, smiled, and engaged in some small talk as he weighed it using his old weighing machine, *"Dekho poore 29.6 kg!"* ("See, it's exactly 29.6 kg!"), he announced confidently.

I couldn't help but notice how he ever so subtly used his knee to support the cylinder as he weighed it. I didn't say a word. Instead, I called out casually, "Please get our weighing machine, will you?"

The delivery boy's face turned pale. He suddenly remembered he had urgent deliveries somewhere else. I gave him an unimpressed look and told him to wait. Out came our brand-new digital weighing machine.

The real fun began. I set the cylinder on our digital scale, and lo and behold - it read 26.4 kg. More than 3 kg short! The delivery boy stuttered, suddenly questioning the accuracy of my weighing machine. But when I mentioned filing an official complaint with all the evidence I had gathered, he quickly changed his tune.

"Let me get another one from the lorry," he said, voice trembling with respect.

I watched from the balcony as he frantically checked one cylinder after another, weighing each with his vintage contraption, until finally, he found one that passed the test and came back to deliver it to me. This time, I didn't even feel the need to weigh it. To my surprise, that cylinder lasted a whole month!

From then on, the delivery boy always showed up with a new, calibrated weighing machine, even going as far as requesting me to weigh the cylinder myself.

Looking back, I think I did my duty as a responsible citizen. Had I ignored the problem, I'd probably still be grumbling about it today. As my wife pointed out later, "Why don't you issue an advisory from the RWA?"

I imagined it for a moment - a full-blown resident debate, fingers pointing in every direction, everyone somehow bashing the RWA for each underweight cylinder in the city. Ah, another Pandora's box! Some things are best kept light and just handled with a smile.

15

CHAPTER SEVEN

WHEN THE MYSTERY SQUEAK TURNED INTO A RAT-TASTROPHE

It had been about five months since we had moved into our flat when it happened. Winter had settled in completely, with its frosty grip making every day feel a little colder. To add to the seasonal joys, two of our neighbours - above and below - had embarked on full-scale renovation projects. The constant symphony of tile cutters, wood planers, and the voices of workers filled the air at all times, even with the doors tightly shut. Opening windows was out of the question, thanks to the biting cold.

"I hear this strange biting noise every now and then in my kitchen," my wife complained one day, her eyebrows arched with concern.

"It's nothing but the renovation work," I reassured her confidently. What else could it be?

But she remained uneasy. Every other day, she would say, "Why don't I hear this noise in any other room?"

"That's because you keep the kitchen window open while you're working," I explained, spinning an impromptu theory about acoustics. She seemed convinced - maybe it was my engineering degree that gave the theory a bit more weight.

We'd always made it a point to spray pesticides in our homes every year, no matter where we lived. Somehow, in all the moving chaos, we had forgotten to do it in our new flat. That was until my wife spotted a silverfish in one of the cupboards. Alarmed, she turned to me urgently, "We need to call pest control. We're already late!"

And that's how I found myself dialing 'Sunshine Pest Control' in Sector 65, Mohali. That very afternoon, two men showed up, dressed in gear that made them look like astronauts about to embark on a moon mission. They carried spray guns, satchels with chemicals, and wore masks covering their faces. I handed them a bucket and some water, and they quickly got to work.

Room by room, cupboard by cupboard, they left no corner unsprayed. All the drain holes, bed boxes, and lofts were treated. It took them nearly an hour to finish the entire flat. The kitchen, however, was the ultimate frontier.

With military precision, they began in the kitchen, moving from under the sink to the top cabinets. They finally reached the loft that concealed the exhaust pipe of the chimney - just a few empty jute baskets and plastic containers were stored there. As one of the guys climbed the ladder to spray inside, the mystery of the strange noises my wife had heard was dramatically solved.

The moment he opened the cabinet, out popped a rat, almost the size of a kitten! The pest control guy let out a shout and nearly toppled off the ladder, while the rat scurried for cover, as if performing some magician's disappearing act. He quickly gathered his courage, aimed the spray gun, but the rat had already vanished into some unseen crevice. He then placed rodent-repelling cakes in the cabinet and covered the outlet of the exhaust pipe with a wire mesh to prevent future intrusions.

We were told to keep all windows and doors shut for two hours, so we found ourselves bundled up in the balcony. My wife, triumphant, couldn't resist poking fun at my "expert" knowledge about renovation noises. And honestly, she deserved the victory lap.

While we laughed about it, the real question dawned on us: How did a rat manage to reach the seventh floor? The answer hit me immediately - those darn ducts that carry all the piping! The rat must have climbed up the duct, finding its way to my flat and sneaking through the exhaust pipe reached the kitchen's loft.

A lesson well learnt - keep the ducts closed, always. Besides, open ducts don't exactly add to the aesthetic charm of a building.

And, not surprisingly, once the new RWA took over, one of their first instructions was to keep the ducts shut at all times. Of course, in our Society, whether anyone listens is another story altogether!

LEANING TOWER OF OUR SOCIETY THAT WASN'T!

Once, I arrived a bit late to a rather serious RWA meeting. This was odd, as our discussions usually started on a lighter note. As I stepped in, I caught one of the members passionately stating, "I agree, a structural audit of all the buildings in our Society must be done. We must write to the AWHO at the earliest. We aren't feeling safe after the flood fury," he said, and the President nodded in agreement.

Perplexed, I asked, "What's the case here? Why aren't we safe?"

It turned out that a few residents were demanding this audit after the recent floods that wreaked havoc in our Society. With confidence, I assured the room, "I've had plenty of experience in infrastructure development. There won't be any structural issue with these buildings - they're designed to cater for such loads and stresses."

Drawing on my experience with MES buildings, I explained, "They're structurally robust, even if they do lack some finishing touches. Look at the Bhuj earthquake - civilian buildings suffered massive damage, but the MES ones stood strong."

My words didn't quite sway my RWA friends, so a letter was still sent to AWHO, requesting a structural audit. Soon enough, a curt response arrived, echoing exactly what I had said earlier : "The buildings were designed by structural engineers and vetted by competent authorities. They already include a safety factor for natural calamities like floods and earthquakes." A classic shut-up letter.

Still curious, I wondered aloud, "Who initiated this demand, anyway?" Turns out, it was our very own resident Mr ABC, known for his, shall we say, creative concerns.

Going back in time, in July 2023, unprecedented floods hit our area. The entire Society was underwater - basements flooded, cars floating, and even ground-floor residents stranded. For nearly 10 days, there was no power or water. Panic set in, and amidst the chaos, boats were ferried in to help move residents from place to place. Through it all, the RWA managed the situation impressively.

But then, one morning, chaos erupted near 'T' Tower. Standing knee-deep in water, Mr ABC was shouting, "This tower has tilted! The others will follow soon!" Alarmed, people gathered, and the RWA members rushed over to assess the situation. After a thorough check, no tilt was found, but Mr ABC's words left a lasting fear among some.

Once the waters receded and life returned to normal, I bumped into Mr ABC during my evening walk. Something was different about him. "Looking sharp with those new glasses, when did you start wearing them?" I asked.

With a straight face, he replied, "I went for an eye check-up. The doctor said I had parallax in my eyes and prescribed these glasses."

Parallax. And there it was - the mystery of the tilting tower solved. I couldn't help but laugh. It all made sense now, and I chuckled even more thinking of my friends who had taken his word as gospel and even demanded a structural audit!

CHAPTER NINE

HYDRAULICS GONE AWRY DURING OUR SOCIETY FLOODS

In July 2023, our Society was caught in the fury of a flood, all due to four days of relentless rain. While the residents of Site 1 valiantly blocked water entry points with anything they could find, Site 2 faced a different fate altogether.

As boats ferried residents to and fro, our streets transformed into a surreal waterway, knee-deep in murky water. Fortunately, the personal networks of the RWA members came to the rescue. An army of engineers arrived at lightning speed, armed with pumping sets and sandbags, while fire tenders joined the fray - all for the sake of our residents.

Once the rain finally stopped, the real challenge began: how to pump out the water that surrounded us like an unwelcome guest, with three to four feet of standing water everywhere.

"Why don't we just start the pumps?" some residents fumed, their drenched t-shirts clinging to their skin as they stormed the RWA office. We were in serious strategizing mode, desperate to restore normalcy as soon as possible.

"We have all the pumps ready and connected to a generator. So what's the holdup? Just start them and pump the water out!"

insisted one resident, dressed a bit better than the rest, his broken English accented with a typical Punjabi flair. We were impressed by his calmness but equally baffled by his insistence.

"But the water is everywhere!" we argued. "You know, water maintains its level. No matter how much we pump, it will come back through all the open entry points. We have to wait it out..."

"No, no! The ground outside is much lower," he insisted. "I've lived here for a while, so I know the topography well. We can pump it out!" His confidence left us scratching our heads.

To appease the increasingly irate crowd, we followed him to the pumping site for further clarification. But to our surprise, the 'Professor' had vanished, likely avoiding the embarrassment of his confusing theories.

"Professor ji kithe hain?" (Translation: Where is the Professor?) his friend, who had accompanied him to the office, asked, bewildered.

"Where is the Professor?" we echoed, incredulous. What subject could he possibly teach?

As we waded back through the water, we could only hope he didn't teach hydraulics at any college. The thought of future engineers trying to pump water from a submerged island was enough to make anyone chuckle - if only the rain would stop for good!

CHAPTER TEN

WHEN DOG POOP POLICIES MET MILITARY RANKS

It was just two months since the new RWA took charge, but it already felt like we'd been dropped into a whirlwind of challenges. From learning the intricacies of society rules to addressing resident complaints, our daily sessions often stretched beyond lunch. We were on a mission to improve the Society, and no obstacle - however small - would deter us. We'd been elected for this, after all.

Of all the issues we faced, one stood out: dog poop. It seemed like everywhere we turned, there it was - in the parks, on the roads, even in the lifts! Despite the growing chorus of complaints, many residents turned a blind eye to the culprits. Determined to take action, we made dog poop management a priority. Strict fines were announced, and dog owners were urged to carry poop collectors and take their pets outside the Society for relieving them. Inter-site dog walking (our Society had two sites) was banned to prevent smart rule-breakers from playing hide-and-seek with us.

To our delight, the dog poop situation improved. Inter-site dog walking incidents plummeted, and things were starting to look up. That is, until she entered the scene.

One morning, a security guard approached us, frustration etched on his face. "Sir, we've been stopping people from walking dogs between the sites, but there's one lady who just won't listen. She argues every time!"

"Inform her to visit office tomorrow," we replied, bracing ourselves for a conversation.

The next day at sharp 11, in walked the lady - calm, but clearly not in the mood for pleasantries. She sat before the President, and before anyone could say a word, the questions flew : "Why can't I walk my dog to the other site? I've lived here forever, and no one's ever stopped me! Aren't we free to do what we want? And your security guard - how dare he?"

The President, ever the diplomat, patiently explained the new rules and how they benefited the whole Society. He emphasized that residents could move freely between sites, but not with their dogs. This, he clarified, was to stop people from letting their dogs relieve themselves in the other site. Simple and fair, we thought.

But the lady wasn't having it. "No, no. How can I go anywhere without my dog? My dog is always with me. I don't let my dog relieve itself anywhere but in my own site!" she declared, her anger rising.

One RWA member tried to step in. "Please, could you show some respect and understand the President's point of view?"

Big mistake.

Her eyes locked onto him like a heat-seeking missile. "Don't you know who I am? I work in the corporate world, and I was a CAPTAIN before that. Don't you dare try to teach me!" she shouted.

Stunned, we tried to offer tea to cool the situation, but she stormed out before the cup even hit the saucer.

After she left, we sat in silence, trying to recall the hierarchy of military ranks - Captain, Major, Colonel, Brigadier, General... had something changed since our retirement? After all, many of us sitting there had risen to much higher military ranks ... had been colonels, brigadiers, even generals. We could only smile at the irony!!!

As I reflected on the incident, I couldn't help but wonder: Why does ego so often get in the way of common sense? Why can't we set it aside for the greater good? It's a mystery that, like the dog poop, we continue to step around.

25

CHAPTER ELEVEN

THE SOLAR DREAM : FROM GREEN TO GLARE

In our lively Society, a peculiar paradox unfolded during one RWA meeting as members brainstormed ways to cut costs while embracing energy conservation. "We must advance towards energy conservation. A solar power system would prove a boon for our Society, where 25% of our expenditure goes towards electricity tariffs," declared one informed member, igniting the team's enthusiasm.

Yet, as excitement built, the practicality of the plan began to surface. "But where will we put up massive solar panels? Do we even have adequate space? And what about the investment cost?" asked a tech-savvy member, expressing legitimate concerns without entirely dismissing the idea.

Despite the questions, the majority rushed to approve the initiative, eager to impress the residents and perhaps to prove a point. "Let's call in the experts! Don't worry about the funds; we'll manage somehow," the President announced, instilling a sense of optimism.

Before long, the experts arrived, and everyone listened with rapt attention during their presentation - a rarity in past meetings! They discussed the advantages of solar systems, how quickly panels could be erected, and their ease of integration with the grid. The RWA members exchanged glances, convinced that this project would secure their next term in office.

However, curiosity soon sparked another round of questions. "Where will we put up the solar panels, and will the energy produced suffice for our Society?" I eagerly asked. The expert deflected with a counter-question, "How much electricity do you consume now?"

The Estate Manager, who was no stranger to the numbers, chimed in, "We pay around 7 lakh for electricity every month, consuming 70 K2W." Both he and I shared a sense of intrigue about the expert's proposed locations for the massive panels. "We can easily deploy them on rooftops of all the towers, community centers, and even some small substations that you have. The roof of our Society Shopping Centre is also available," he explained.

"But our towers' roofs are filled with hot water systems," I pointed out. One member quickly responded, "Those heating systems are non-functional. We can clear them out to make room for solar panels!"

Despite the enthusiasm, doubts lingered. Would the project truly be beneficial in the long run with its huge initial investment coupled with high maintenance cost, and could it meet our energy needs? After further discussions, the experts clarified that most of our energy consumption came from water supply systems and elevators, while lighting of common areas consumed far less power. They estimated that deploying all the suggested solar panels could save about 40% of our electricity costs.

Excitedly, members pulled out calculators, imagining the savings like rabbits pulled from a hat. But when the numbers were crunched, the results were less than thrilling: a mere 10 paisa saved per square foot. We thanked the experts and promised to consider their proposal.

In the days that followed, the dream of solar panels lingered in my mind - scattered across the Society, reflecting the sun's rays and creating a glassy landscape instead of the vibrant greenery we cherished, all for the meager savings of just 10 paisa.

I couldn't help but wonder: why not just install stand-alone solar panels for our perimeter lighting? If we're going to embrace solar energy, let's at least do it in a way that reflects our community spirit! Sometimes, it seems, our grand ambitions overshadow what truly makes our neighbourhood shine.

CHAPTER TWELVE

A Misadventure in Home Decor

On a bright winter morning, my wife and I were lounging on our Society lawn, soaking in the sunshine. We were deep in conversation, plotting our strategy to entertain some important family guests arriving soon. The itinerary was unfolding - places to visit, dining spots to hit, and everything in between. My wife was particularly fixated on the fact that during our last visit to Pune, our hosts had rolled out the red carpet for us. They even whisked us away to the holy land of Shirdi, making our stay unforgettable.

"I want everything to be perfect this time," she insisted, her eyes sparkling with determination. "We need to vacuum the house, set out our finest linen, and - oh! We have to fix that painting in the balcony. It looks so bare!"

Ah yes, the painting. Just days before, a storm had decided to unleash its fury, turning our balcony into a battlefield. Our beloved hand-painted souvenir - a small but sentimental piece depicting a historical war memorial - had taken a tumble from the wall and shattered.

As we were engrossed in our drama, our tower friend sauntered over, his curiosity piqued by our conversation.

"Have you ever been to Kharar Market?" he asked, a twinkle in his eye. "It's one of the oldest markets around! Needles, bags, you name it - everything is available at unbelievable prices!"

This caught my wife's attention immediately. "Is there anyone who can fix the painting?" she asked eagerly.

Our friend, sensing an opportunity for some entertaining gossip (his wife was out of town, after all), launched into an elaborate description of Kharar Market. "Just head towards Bhuru Chowk," he said, waving his hands animatedly. "Turn right, and you'll find a shop where the owner is a miracle worker. He's done wonders for me at rock-bottom prices!"

With my wife's excitement palpable, I knew we had to make a move - immediately after lunch.

Kharar Market is notoriously chaotic, so we opted for my trusty Jawa Classic motorbike. With my wife perched behind me, we donned our helmets and set off. Let me tell you, it was quite a sight - two serious riders on a bike, with one of them holding a shattered piece of art like a trophy!

Navigating the streets was easy, and in less than 15 minutes, we found ourselves in front of the shop our friend had talked about.

I parked my prized bike and approached the shop. The owner looked welcoming. *"Mujhe yahan Mr ABC ne bheja hai, is painting ka shisha toot gaya hai, use badalvana hai,"* I explained. (Translation: "Mr ABC from our Society sent me here because the glass of my painting is broken.")

The shopkeeper perked up a little, recognizing my friend's name. He scribbled my details on the back of the painting, inspecting the damage. *"Iska frame bhi badalna padega, shisha fit karte waqt who toot sakta hai,"* he advised. (Translation: "You'll need a new frame too; the old one might break while fitting the glass.")

I hesitated, the old frame was perfect - it matched the painting and was part of the charm. But his sales pitch was persuasive, and against my better judgment, I agreed citing a condition that new frame had to be exactly as the present one.

"Come back in an hour!" I told my wife confidently.

"Actually, it'll be ready in a week," he corrected, casually. My wife's expression turned stormy. "A week? Our guests will be here soon!" she protested. I soothed her, suggesting we leave the painting and hoping for the best.

Days turned into a blur. Guests came and went, and when the call finally came from the shopkeeper, we were less than thrilled. After a long wait, we arrived at the shop to collect our masterpiece.

But horror struck! The once-historical war memorial painting was now encased in a jazzy frame that seemed to mock its solemnity. To make matters worse, the shopkeeper charged us a whopping 1200 bucks for what I believed was a 500-rupee job. We begrudgingly paid, accepting our fate, and left the shop with our bizarre new decoration.

Now, every time I glance at that painting, it reminds me of my friend's enthusiastic endorsement, the shopkeeper's indifferent attitude, and the unfortunate final product. Guests inevitably comment on it, and I seize the opportunity to launch into the story of our epic painting adventure, all while secretly wishing I could replace that ridiculous frame.

So, do I ever mention this episode to my tower friend? No, some tales are best left untold - it might hurt somebody's sentiments!

CHAPTER THIRTEEN

NAME BOARDS AND NERVOUSNESS UNLIMITED

"Why don't you plan to visit us? It's been so long since we last met. I can assure you'll get some good ideas for your Society," my daughter urged over the phone.

It had been a while since we visited her, so we quickly set our plans in motion and booked a direct return flight to Pune for a three-day stay. Little did I know, this trip would inspire a chain of events back home in our Society.

Our time in Pune was filled with laughter, gossip, and catching up. But amidst the fun, my eyes were constantly scouting for ideas I could bring back for our Society. One visit in particular caught my attention - 'Package type STP' in my daughter's posh society. No odour, everything was neat, organized, and polished. As if I didn't know it! They even had beautifully designed name boards at the entrance of each tower, displaying names and even ranks of the defence personnel residing there. It added such grace and pride to the place.

Returning home, I couldn't help but share my insights. "Why don't we put up 'Name Boards' in all our towers, showcasing residents' names? It'll enhance the Society's image and bring a sense of pride," I suggested during an RWA meeting. The idea sparked curiosity, but one member quickly raised concerns, "What about security? With names displayed, won't it pose a risk?"

"Sir, we proudly flaunt regiment logos on our cars. Where does security go then?" I countered, a bit puzzled by the concern.

After a few more rounds of deliberation, the RWA gave a nod to the idea. A flex board vendor was brought in, and we designed a sample Name Board, even discussing the flexibility to change names or ranks if needed. The vendor was given an advance, and soon, the first board was up at the entrance of one tower. It looked fantastic - names and ranks shining in gold, elevating the tower's stature.

The excitement quickly spread across the Society. Residents of other towers came by to admire it. "No more guessing who's who in the tower! It fosters camaraderie," some remarked.

But no good deed goes unpunished. Our Society WhatsApp Group soon lit up with messages. Some appreciated the idea, while others were bogged down with security concerns. A few even quibbled over whether names should be full, cryptic, or decorated.

The RWA took a balanced view, asking each resident how they'd prefer their names to appear. One member even volunteered to approach every household. After painstakingly gathering everyone's preferences, we were ready to place the final order. Or so we thought.

Just when it seemed the project was on track, a curveball came. "Shouldn't we spend this money elsewhere, on a better project?" someone suggested. When asked how much money and what project exactly, there was only silence. But the damage was done - progress stalled or shall I say the confused RWA?

However, I didn't give up. We took the proposal to the AGBM, where it was unanimously endorsed. Victory! The Name Boards would soon be a reality...

Still, the whole experience left me reflecting - why do we get so tangled up in unfounded fears? Especially when all our names and details are already public via apps like MyGate. Isn't promoting camaraderie and enhancing our Society's brand worth a small cost?

Passing by a posh villa in Panchkula after a round of golf that proudly displayed rank, name, decoration and regiment of its resident, I couldn't help but think, maybe we're just overthinking this whole 'security' thing.

In the end, it wasn't about the Name Board - it was about pride in our community.

CHAPTER FOURTEEN

REFUGE AREA OR REFUSE AREA? A COMEDY OF CLUTTER

The RWA had been tirelessly reminding residents about the ACs dripping water all over. The cause? A simple disconnected drain pipe. The consequences? Mold, ugly facades, damage to building structure, and potential health hazards - especially for children and the elderly. The appeal was simple: "Get it fixed. Society plumbers are available to help." Yet, hardly anyone listened.

As complaints poured in, the RWA had to adopt a sterner approach. But, in our Society, enforcing rules can be a dangerous game. No one wants to get caught in the crossfire between individual liberties and communal responsibilities. So, the RWA turned to the residents, requesting them to talk to their neighbours.

Now, I decided to do my part. It seemed like a simple task: politely ask a neighbour in our tower to fix their dripping AC. Given the possibility that the resident could be a single lady, I convinced my wife to accompany me. We took the stairs - after all, it wasn't a long climb.

After a few rings, a young guy opened the door, casually dressed and clearly reluctant to entertain visitors. I asked him about the AC.

"There's a dripping AC in your flat. Would you mind fixing it? It's causing some trouble down below."

The boy shrugged. "Oh, that's not my room. It's the other guy's. I'll tell him tonight when he comes back."

I was more puzzled by the situation than annoyed. Rooms in the same flat rented out to different people? The stories of subletting in our Society seemed to be true after all!

Before leaving, I glanced over at the common area nearby, to be the so-called "Refuge Area" - intended to serve as a safe spot during emergencies. What I saw was jaw-dropping: scattered pots, empty cartons, garbage, and the unmistakable stench of dog urine. Not an inch of space left.

I turned back to the boy. "Why is all this here? This area is meant to be kept clear - it's for emergencies."

He merely shrugged again. "Everyone dumps stuff here. Even the maids don't bother cleaning it."

I left the place feeling more disappointed than I expected. Over the next few days, I kept discussing it with my wife. Why were some residents so indifferent, blatantly ignoring society rules? Everyone knew the importance of a clear refuge area.

My wife, sensing my frustration, suddenly smiled. "Maybe they misunderstood 'refuge area' as 'refuse area'," she said, trying to lighten the mood.

But her joke brought home a real point - what kind of society are we shaping if we don't follow the basics of community living? Ugly green cloths flapping over balconies, clothes hanging over railings, common spaces turned into dumping grounds - are these things that require RWA enforcement? Can't we just exercise a bit of common sense?

It makes one wonder: do we deserve a better living environment if we're not ready to do our bit? Maybe, just maybe, the real "fix" needed isn't just for the ACs - it's for our attitudes.

CHAPTER FIFTEEN

THE NEVER-ENDING WI-FI STRUGGLE

"Which network service is better here?" came a message from a new resident in our Society's WhatsApp Group. A harmless enough question - innocent, even - considering the minefield they were stepping into. I sat back with my phone, ready to give my two cents when my wife, engrossed in a heated debate on Times Now, shot me a warning look. "Think before you write anything," she advised wisely.

She was right, of course. Our history with network service providers had been nothing short of disastrous. I paused, reconsidered my response, but couldn't resist the temptation to be brutally honest. "The choice is between the devil and the deep sea," I typed out, smug with my witty remark. But as soon as I hit send, I realized I might be pushing my cynicism a bit too far. I deleted it almost as quickly.

Responses soon trickled in - some vouching for Airtel, others for Jio. The opinion was, as expected, split down the middle. But deep down, I suspected none of them were truly satisfied with their own choices. In fact, had I left my message, it wouldn't have been too far off the mark. Sighing, I put my phone down and turned back to the news.

But that brief exchange sent me spiraling down the memory lane, when my wife and I had just moved into this place. Ah, we too were wide-eyed optimists, searching for the best network provider.

"Airtel is excellent here! You won't face any issues," one of our well-meaning neighbours had said. Buoyed by their assurance, I quickly called the Airtel representative. It was as if the guy had been sitting on his bike, waiting for our call. He arrived in record time with his technician, laid out a buffet of plans, and after some insight, we chose one.

"I want my laptop to run smoothly, no lag. I'll be working from the master bedroom," I informed him.

"Netflix and Prime Video are my priorities," my wife chimed in, shooting me a look as if daring me to contest the hierarchy.

The technician nodded with all the confidence. "No problem, Ma'am and Sir. This modem will give you top signals in every room. Guaranteed." He set it up in our living room, did a speed test, and off he went. My wife, pleased with the promptness, signed up for the full-year plan, one free month as a bonus.

Within days, my laptop started struggling for a signal. "Don't worry, you don't use it much anyway," my wife said, in a tone that suggested I could just as well work from the moon. Grudgingly, I moved to the living room. Then, her beloved Netflix began troubling. And, just like that, the tech guy was back, fixing things every few days, muttering cryptic excuses like, "Your TV is old, Ma'am. It doesn't catch the signal well."

That was the wrong thing to say. "Three months old Sony Bravia isn't ancient!" she fumed, chasing him out with a tirade that left him speechless. By the end of the year, we waved goodbye to Airtel with the same relief one feels after narrowly escaping quicksand.

Enter Jio, our new knight in shining armour. The representative confidently said, "Sir, just place the modem higher, and there will be no issues." Odd advice, but at this point, we were willing to try anything. The modem moved up, and for a few days, it worked like a charm. Then came the déjà vu - spotty signals, buffering marathons. "Maybe the original spot was better," the guy admitted sheepishly, moving the modem back to its former position.

This time, we played it smart - or so we thought - opting for a three-month plan. Within that short period, Jio managed to test every ounce of our patience. One day, the guy suggested, "You'll need a range extender if you want coverage in all rooms." An extender meant cables, and cables meant holes in the walls - no thanks.

And so, we've resigned ourselves to this new normal. I now often work in the living room, tethered to the modem like a ship to its anchor, while my wife practices the art of patience, enduring buffering breaks every 20 minutes during her Netflix binges. It's a forced intermission, really. A break neither of us asked for but have begrudgingly come to accept.

A few days later, a new message popped up in the Group: "BSNL is setting up a stall in the complex to share their new plans. Everyone is welcome!"

I couldn't control my laughter. Another contender? We're officially spoiled for choice... or doomed to repeat the same saga. The spinning wheel of buffering would still be our constant companion. Ah, the joys of modern connectivity!!

CHAPTER SIXTEEN

The Maintenance Mayhem : Emails, Excuses and Power Cut Threats

"Why should I pay the monthly maintenance fees when I'm not staying there?" snapped a furious flat owner at our Society President on his mobile phone. He wasn't alone either - several other defaulters voiced the same frustration, every now and then. It seemed like a mutiny was brewing over maintenance fees!

One day, during an RWA meeting, we gathered to review the long list of maintenance fee defaulters. When the Treasurer pulled out the list, it was so long it practically rolled across the room. We were speechless. The list included everyone from those a few months behind to those whose dues had practically aged into relics. The total amount owed? Well, let's just say it could probably fund a small island.

"We need to act!" declared one member, and everyone chimed in, "Yes, yes, send a final email warning them!" A sternly worded draft was prepared, and off it went to all the defaulters. Except...

surprise! I received one too, even though I've never missed a payment. Turns out, they sent it to everyone as a "friendly" heads-up. The result? Mass confusion and a few raised eyebrows. One owner exclaimed, "What a funny way to send an email!" But hey, at least everyone got the message - loud and clear.

Despite the email's dramatic flair, not much happened. At the next review meeting, someone suggested, "Maybe we should call the defaulters personally. They might pay out of guilt!" It seemed like a noble idea, so we split up the list and started dialing away.

The conversations? Oh, they were priceless! "Rent out our flat first," one said. "Improve amenities, then we'll talk!" another quipped. It was like each owner had a ready-made script. While some hung up on us, a few did indeed pay up, probably out of sheer embarrassment. But alas, the list of defaulters still resembled a scroll from a never-ending saga.

As the AGBM approached, we realized we had to face the music. The Treasurer, presented the year's budget with a sprinkle of optimism, highlighting the RWA's attempts to collect dues. But the crowd was in no mood for gentle words. "Why don't we just cut their backup power and suspend MyGate access?" an owner suggested. The room erupted in applause. Clearly, they wanted action.

With newfound courage, we flashed a bold message on the LED screen outside the RWA office: "Clear dues within a fortnight or lose backup power and MyGate access!" An email, this time targeted only at the defaulters, was dispatched as well.

A month later, during a power outage, my wife casually mentioned, "That one defaulter is still enjoying backup power. What happened to the tough talk?" Surprised, I quickly called the Estate Manager. His response? "Sir, I'm waiting for orders from the President." Shocked again! My wife wasn't impressed, calling the whole thing a grand joke - lots of talk, no follow-through.

Though a bit deflated, I gathered my thoughts and offered some "secret" advice at the next RWA meeting. But that's a story for another day!

CHAPTER SEVENTEEN

WHO KNEW OUR SENIOR CITIZENS COULD TURN BENCH SHIFTING INTO A TEAM SPORT?

At the start of a new tenure, the RWA members gathered for their first meeting, buzzing with ideas to improve the Society. "We must improve existing signage in our Society. There are far too few sign boards," declared one enthusiastic member, waving his hands for emphasis. "You see, society rules convey much better through these boards due to their visibility all the time."

A round of applause erupted, and it was unanimously decided: the first project would be to install new signage throughout the Society. News of the new signage spread among residents like wildfire, and soon, everyone was eagerly awaiting the changes.

To kick things off, a thorough survey was conducted to identify the best spots for the signs - even the basements where the new car parking slots would go were measured. One member, yours truely, prepared a PowerPoint presentation for the RWA, detailing the design of the boards, measurements, color schemes, and captions that conveyed the Society's rules. The presentation was a hit, leaving everyone impressed. With a nod from the President, the project was greenlit.

Next, they called in the flex board vendor. Every detail was explained meticulously to avoid any mishaps. A sample board was produced, and it looked fantastic. The order was placed, focusing particularly on the areas with the most rule violations. "No littering, no flower plucking, park cars properly, no cycling or ball games in the parks, be mindful of dog poop, and the all-important 'No shifting benches in the parks on your own'" were just a few of the critical messages to be displayed.

When the vendor finally delivered the boards, it was time to install them. Some members shied away from this task, but I stepped up, determined to ensure our Society had the signage it needed. After a bit of grouting and hard work, the once-bare Society now shimmered with colorful signs.

On my evening walks, I noticed residents pausing to read the signs, some even chuckling at a few hilarious ones and appreciating the efforts. The RWA was thrilled.

One particular sign caught my eye: "Please don't shift benches on your own." It was strategically placed right behind the sturdy cast-iron benches designed for elderly residents. Despite the numerous permanent benches scattered around, these cast-iron gems were special. Heavy and built for comfort, they were perfect for our community's senior citizens.

All was well until one fateful evening when I took a stroll with my wife to inspect the Society's horticulture. As we wandered, I noticed the signboard still intact but the benches? Displaced! A cluster of three or four benches was positioned facing each other, occupied by a group of elderly ladies engaged in deep conversation.

"Mataji, eh benchan nu apni jagah to shift na kita karo," I said, trying to keep my tone light. (Translation: "Madam, please don't

shift these benches from their place.")

"*Aapan sab ne amne samne baith ke gal karni hondi hai,*" one of the elderly ladies replied with a smile. (Translation: "We need to chat together facing each other.") I sighed and walked away, resolving to remind the security supervisor to keep an eye on those benches.

Days passed, and yet again, the same scene unfolded: benches clustered together, elderly ladies chatting away. This time, curiosity piqued my interest. How could these women possibly move those heavy benches?

As I approached, I couldn't help but ask, "*Dasso ai benchan nu kon roj roj shift karda hai?*" (Translation: "Please tell me who shifts these benches every day?")

The same lady smiled knowingly and replied, "*Ai purani hadian vich aji vi bara jor hai.*" (Translation: "These old bones still have a lot of strength.")

In that moment, I realized I'd never ask them again to keep the benches in place! With that delightful revelation, the benches - and the resilient spirit of our Society - remained just as they were meant to be: a gathering place for laughter, conversation, and the shared stories of life.

CHAPTER EIGHTEEN

THE STRAY WITH A PLAN: A SOCIETY'S STRUGGLE

After the chaos of the July 2023 floods that threw our Society into disarray, life eventually began to return to normal. Amidst the muddy aftermath, I found myself writing an ATR, detailing our shortcomings and, more importantly, the steps we needed to take to protect our Society in the future.

One thing was clear: we had to keep the water out next time. Sandbags were an obvious choice, but they had limitations - they were slow to deploy. Our majestic gates, while grand and strong, had gaps through their iron bars that allowed water to seep right through. So, the Estate Manager took charge of a new plan: weld a metal sheet at the base of each gate to stop the water. And soon, we had what we thought was an impregnable line of defence. Sure, there were still tiny gaps along the sides, but sandbags would fill those in a pinch.

With the gates fortified, all seemed well. The Society was dry, peace reigned, and our carefully patched-up defences seemed untested - until the day a black stray dog appeared inside the Society. He had white paws and a perpetually puzzled expression, wandering around leashless. One baffled resident, seeing it for the first time, asked aloud, "Did someone adopt a stray dog as a pet?"

The stray quickly became a familiar sight, especially in the mornings and evenings. We were used to Labradors, Pomeranians, Dobermans, and even Huskies, strutting around with their owners. But this black dog? No collar, no owner, no regard for the rules. It was a real mystery.

Soon enough, the RWA decided the stray had to go. The security guards were mobilized, and thus began the 'Great Stray Chase' of our Society. The guards, earnest in their mission, raced after this energetic dog around the park, into one tower and out another. It was a spectacle! The dog seemed to treat it like a game, darting left and right, as the guards stumbled after him. Residents watched, some filming and some laughing, sharing the clips on our Society's WhatsApp Group.

After many comical, failed attempts, the RWA decided to regroup. There had to be a secret entrance we hadn't found. After some careful detective work, they found it: those pesky, minor gaps on the sides of the gates. The dog had been sneaking in through them. The gaps were quickly patched up with iron mesh, and a victory was declared. The stray dog was officially evicted.

Or so we thought.

A few mornings later, I opened my door on the seventh floor, and there it was - a mess right in the corridor. Dog poop. I was livid. Who would be so irresponsible? If people can't handle their pets, why even keep them? Determined to solve the mystery, I decided to investigate.

Without CCTV cameras on each floor, my options were limited. I made a mental list of the pet-owning residents. There were only two in my tower: one on the ground floor - a highly disciplined guy I trusted, and the other on my upper floor, who had a Labrador. The pieces started to come together.

I marched up to the upper floor. After several insistent rings, the door finally opened. There stood an elderly person, Labrador barking in the background. He could barely walk without support - let alone take his dog downstairs for a bathroom break. His son had gone out for a few days at work. It seemed like an open and shut case.

I wasted no time in expressing my frustration. I explained the situation, making it clear that the mess needed to be addressed before the RWA stepped in. To my surprise, the old man, entirely unbothered, responded confidently, *"Aithe andar ek kala kutta kumda hai, ai kam oda hai"* (Translation: "A black dog roams around inside, it is certainly his doing").

I countered, *"Paaji, jadon di asi gate te jali banni hai, kuta nahi aaya, tussi apne kute nu control karo"* (Translation: "Since we sealed all the gate openings, that stray hasn't entered. You should control your dog").

As I walked back, the absurdity of the situation started to sink in, and I couldn't help but laugh. Was it really plausible that the stray had sneaked into the building, made it up seven floors, just to relieve himself in our corridor? It sounded like the start of some ridiculous urban myth.

Who knows, maybe next time someone will claim they saw a cat operating the elevator, riding up, and dropping off its 'special delivery' on a random floor. In this Society, nothing would surprise me anymore!

THE GREAT ROAD CONSTRUCTION CHRONICLES : WHEN BORROW PITS DISAPPEARED LIKE MAGIC

Back in October 2023, our RWA and RWS of Ansals met with one shared mission: to finally conquer the legendary nemesis that had plagued both communities - the infamous road. Cracked, cratered, and practically resembling a lunar surface, this road was the reason for every car's misaligned wheels and every resident's growing frustration. Naturally, fixing it became the top priority. Both groups, under relentless pressure from their respective societies, set out to make the road drivable again.

But fixing the road was no easy task. The road to collaboration itself was filled with bumps and potholes! Design, construction type (paver block, bitumen, hybrid!), cost-sharing, tenders, timelines - each point became a mini battle. The RWA was rich in experience in road construction, while the RWS... well, they were rich in other ways, making communication a challenge. After weeks of back-and-forth, agreements were made. The RWS, being the bigger stakeholder, signed a contract with a local contractor, and everyone braced themselves for construction to begin.

But I, ever the vigilant one, had a nagging concern. "What about the dressing of the central verge and road shoulders with soil?" I asked, thinking of safety and aesthetics. As expected, the contractor shrugged it off, "Sir, don't worry, it will be ensured." But I wasn't convinced and made sure it was part of the contract. I knew where these guys cut corners and made money.

Once construction began, I changed the route of my evening walks from within our Society to along the road, purely out of curiosity (and maybe to see things were going smoothly). Paver blocks started going in, but I noticed something was off. No soil filling, no berm dressing, just bare, sad-looking road shoulders. Day after day, the contractor dodged my questions about the soil filling, with his usual "Sir, don't worry, we'll import fresh soil at the end, and fill up all the borrow pits." Sure, I thought, likely as snow in summer.

As the months dragged on, construction was almost done, but not a speck of fresh soil had touched those road shoulders. The borrow pits, debris and neglected patches were still there, clear as day, while the contractor seemed to have vanished into thin air, perhaps busy digging elsewhere. Days rolled and one evening, during my now regular evening walk, I bumped into a particularly outspoken RWS member.

"Hey, what's the status of the soil dressing on the central divider and shoulders?" I asked, expecting the usual excuses. But his response left me speechless: *"Sir, jane do abb. Khadde nazar thodi aa rahe hain. Sari jagah ghaas hi ghaas hai!"* ("Sir, leave it now. No borrow pits are visible anymore. It's all green with grass everywhere!")

And there it was - nature had stepped in where the contractor had failed. Wild shrubs and grass had grown all over, hiding every flaw. The borrow pits had vanished under a layer of green camouflage, making the road look... presentable, at least from a distance. But come the winter again, will the borrow pits re-appear? Anyone guess? Certainly.

CHAPTER TWENTY

THE GREAT SPEED BREAKER SAGA: WHEN ROAD CONSTRUCTION MET COMEDY

A few months ago, in a seemingly ordinary RWA WhatsApp Group - where secrets of the universe (or just our Society) were discussed - I received yet another message from the President. A special meeting was scheduled with members of RWS Ansals to finally tackle the long-delayed road construction project. For weeks, we had gone around in circles, debating pavement designs, alignments, cost sharing and tendering. Yet somehow, every meeting derailed into an intense obsession with - of all things - speed breakers.

"I swear, if I hear one more word about speed breakers, I might break something myself!" I muttered. But sure enough, the moment the meeting began, an RWS member eagerly piped up, "Sir, let's decide on the location of the speed breakers first."

I sighed. "Let's focus on the important things first, like the actual road."

Despite my advice on cost-efficient bituminous roads, the RWS, guided by some mysterious "expert" and perhaps his agenda-driven contractor friend, pushed for interlocking concrete blocks. Eventually, a compromise was reached - a blend of paver blocks and bitumen. And so, construction began, with the contractor promising a speedy three-month completion. I chuckled. I knew better.

As work progressed, the topic of speed breakers followed me everywhere - even on my evening walks. The RWS members seemed obsessed, asking me day in and day out about their placement. So much so, I had to alter my walking route just to avoid the inevitable question.

After much back and forth, I proposed a sensible solution: permanent speed breakers only at critical points, and a few flexible plastic ones elsewhere. But no, RWS wanted permanent speed breakers at every junction. Apparently for RWS, children were playing on the road, and young drivers were racing like it was Formula 1. I couldn't help but laugh.

When bituminous construction finally ended after nine months as against a three-month promise, our President drove on the newly laid road, only to encounter a speed breaker every 50 meters. "Is this an obstacle course?" he exclaimed, baffled by the sheer number of them. The residents of the Ansals were equally perplexed. The RWS members were nowhere to be seen now.

Realizing their error, the RWS swiftly removed most of the speed breakers, much faster than they had built them. Eventually, they followed the original plan I had suggested all along, but only after learning the hard way that speed breakers can't solve every problem.

And that's how life often unfolds, doesn't it? We erect our own barriers, believing they'll safeguard us, only to discover they hinder us more than help. Sometimes, it's only after stumbling that we realize the path was never as perilous as we imagined.

CHAPTER TWENTY-ONE

TRAFFIC JAMS, TOWERS, AND TRUTH BOMBS : MY JOURNEY OF REALIZATION!

It was a typical Saturday, and once again, I found myself behind the wheel, heading to 3B2 market in Mohali. My wife adored it; me? Not so much. What should've been a breezy 10-kilometer drive often turned into a test of patience, especially due to the notorious Landran Chowk. This time, the usual 20 minutes felt more like 40, as I navigated through the chaos.

Even after three hours of shopping, my wife's disappointment was evident, maybe due to her choice of items that weren't there. She was terribly off-mood, and I could feel my hopes for a peaceful dinner fading faster than a good golf ball in a water hazard.

Desperate to lighten the mood, I suggested, "Nothing like some old classic Hindi music for the drive home!" But that backfired - she promptly turned off the YouTube. Switching tactics, I began venting. "From the Judicial Courts junction, it feels like we're entering a no-man's land! Look at this road! The MLA says no berms, yet there aren't even streetlights! It's dangerous!"

Silence. Undeterred, I continued, "They promised a golf course, but all we've got are traffic jams and potholes! Look at this mess!"

As we approached Landran Chowk, the chaos peaked. Cars, trucks, bikes, and even stray animals fought for road space. "Is this a video game? Because dodging everything feels like the main mission!" I joked, trying to make light of it.

From the Chowk, we turned to head for our Society, only to be greeted by tractors and autos coming at us from the wrong side. "Is this normal town planning?" I exclaimed. The bridge leading to our Society was worse - garbage was strewn everywhere. "Looks like a new dumping scheme. Clearly, *'Punjab da Puttar'* isn't staying on this planet!"

Finally when we reached the main gate of our Society, I thought the hard part was over - wrong again. My wife was ready with her critique. "Those fountains? Just for decoration? And the internal roads? Didn't the AGBM approve resurfacing them two months ago?"

I gulped, "Well, these things take time..."

"And the towers!" she pressed on. "Peeling plaster, balconies wrapped in green cloth, and dilapidated entrances! The pool and the squash court? Still under repairs after two years! I've seen hotels build pools on the 100th floor faster!"

Just when I thought I could recover, she dropped the final truth bomb: "You spent the whole trip criticizing the civil administration, something that is beyond your control. But what has your beloved RWA done, something that is within its control? With all their resources, why does our Society still look like this?"

I stammered, "Uh, well, these things take time... and the RWA is working on it..."

As we pulled into our parking slot, I knew I'd lost this round.

Later that night, it hit me: if I had focused on the positives during the drive, I could've avoided her critique. So, I decided to embrace a new approach: a bit of positivity goes a long way! Instead of complaining, I'll celebrate the little things - like the wonderful company I have and the cozy home in a serene place we've built together. Who knew a little optimism could smooth out a bumpy ride?

55

CHAPTER TWENTY-TWO

When in Doubt, Let Kelly Win!

Who doesn't love a sprawling, manicured lawn with flower beds bursting with colour? Our Society was no different. At least, everyone loved to talk about it. Our horticulture was something we were proud of - a landscape designed with expert care when our Society came to life seven years ago. Hedges, gardens, and flower beds all arranged perfectly. In one of the Society quadrangles, there was a long and wide flower bed - a beauty with Kelly plants, their vibrant red and yellow flowers bringing charm to its surroundings.

But like a never-ending Indian TV serial, horticulture took a backseat, replaced by the drama of manpower issues. The horticulture agency could hardly keep a straight schedule, and our once-perfect landscape slowly fell into neglect. The grass turned brown, hedges looked like the aftermath of a bad haircut, and trees stood there like they'd forgotten their roles in the scenery.

The RWA called upon the residents - "Volunteers, we need you!" - to help save the gardens. And predictably, everyone enthusiastically... stayed silent. Eventually, one brave resident was coaxed into taking up the challenge, and with a twinkle of optimism in his eye, he assured us he'd turn things around.

The plan? Seasonal flowers for winter - wonderful, vibrant flowers! We nodded like a crowd watching an IPL match, cheering him on. But then came the shock. The first casualty? The long bed in the quadrangle, with those beautiful Kelly plants. Out they went, uprooted to make way for the new winter flowers. My wife and I would watch the work during our evening walks, and while she worried, I kept telling myself, "Surely something better is coming."

One day, curiosity got the better of me. "Sir, what do we plan to plant here now that Kelly is history?" I asked the volunteer, who perhaps was receiving guidance from one RWA member behind the scenes. "Ice plants," he said confidently, "They look so charming in winter!" Ice plants?! I couldn't imagine the tiny, three-inch-tall ice plants in place of the lush Kelly bed, surrounded by towering Anarmi hedges. It felt like putting a tiny candle in front of a lighthouse!

"But won't we need an enormous number of ice plants for this bed?" I dared to ask. "No problem, we'll add a row of marigolds too!" he replied. I nodded, though inside my head, the mental calculator was already wondering about this mix and the RWA's budget to support this adventure.

Then, the action suddenly stopped. Manpower vanished, no more spades in sight. The bed lay there - bare, sprinkled generously with cowdung manure, nothing to show up except tall wild grass. No fault of the volunteer, I was sure. But I kept my questions to myself, deciding silence was gold.

Not to be deterred, the RWA called in reinforcements - a talented lady with a solid horticulture background from her days in cantonments. When it's about a lady, everyone nods without hesitation, of course! She entered with grace, escorted by a proud RWA member, and after some greetings and tea, she shared her knowledge on what should've been done. She suggested succulents - sturdy, low maintenance, and able to make the garden "look pretty good."

Operation Succulent began, complete with shovels, axes, and optimistic chatter. Succulents were planted - collected from all over our Society, with a few generously donated by the lady. And for a while, it looked like we had achieved something big for that bed.

But then came "The Great Watering." Every time I passed the bed, I saw water practically flooding it. "Too much love, perhaps?" my wife joked. "At this rate, we'll have succulent flowers floating!"

And then, disaster struck again. The succulents began to decay - death by kindness!! The gardeners disappeared, the agency pointed fingers, and there stood the infamous flower bed: wild grass growing, succulents wilting, and the occasional brave Kelly plant peeking out as if to say, "Miss me?"

Winter came and went, and with it, our succulents. The bed was left to its fate-again filled with tall grass, with Kelly bulbs making their comeback like old heroes in a sequel.

The RWA held another urgent meeting. "Someone has to take responsibility!" they all said, turning to me. There was no avoiding it now.

With a sigh, I rolled up my sleeves and declared, "First order of business: cut out the wild grass, but carefully - don't harm the Kelly sprouts, and maintain the bed regularly. Nothing more, nothing less." The Head Gardener nodded, and as if by magic, the gods smiled upon us, and the Kelly plants flourished.

Soon enough, those vibrant flowers were back, blooming in all their summer glory. And the bed? It was never happier.

THE TALE OF FANS, MUSIC, AND MISSING MAGIC OF OUR SOCIETY ELEVATORS

It all started with our Society lifts. Our once-tranquil Society was slowly being driven to madness by those unpredictable metal boxes. Every other day, without fail, a complaint would ping through the MyGate App.

"I've been stuck in the lift for 15 minutes! I pressed the bell, but nothing happened!" cried one frantic resident who managed to find just enough signal to phone the Estate Manager. After a swift rescue operation (the poor lady was released as if she had just been saved from a life-or-death situation), it became clear that this was no isolated incident.

The news spread in the Society like wildfire. Some lifts swayed dramatically as if auditioning for a disaster film, while others let out creaks so loud they could've been mistaken for a dying whale. Complaints came flooding in, the AMC contractor was dragged to the scene time and time again, but the fixes were always temporary.

The lifts continued their rebellious streak, while the residents braced themselves for the next malfunction.

The RWA, fed up with what was quickly becoming a comedy of errors, took matters into their own hands. "We'll handle this!" they declared. Enter the Lady Head of AMC services, who got a piece of the RWA's collective mind. After some stern negotiation, it was agreed that one lift would be perfected as a demo. If it passed the test, all the other lifts would follow suit.

Three days later, a crowd gathered around the demo lift like a group of scientists about to witness a groundbreaking experiment. And lo and behold, the lift worked! Smooth as silk, silent as a whisper, and no swaying at all. Even the emergency systems worked without a hitch, proving that this was indeed a lift you could trust. Bystanders applauded like they'd just seen a magician pull a rabbit out of a hat.

Satisfied, the RWA gave the company the go-ahead to fix the rest of the lifts. For the next month, technicians busied themselves in the towers, and slowly but surely, the lift complaints dwindled. The residents' confidence returned, and the Estate Manager could finally relax. The lifts, it seemed, had been tamed.

Or so we thought.

One afternoon, I hopped into the lift in my tower, only to feel like I'd stepped into an oven. The fans weren't working, and I found myself longing for a breeze. "Time to file a complaint," I thought, tapping away on the MyGate App. Two days later, word reached me that the fans had been fixed. Problem solved, right? Wrong.

The next time I used the lift, the fans were indeed working, but they sounded like they'd been replaced with jet engines. The noise was so loud. I called up the Estate Manager, who calmly explained that the noisy fans were a "known issue." The lifts, he said, would be fine-tuned later.

"Fine," I sighed. "But what about the music? It used to play softly in here, and now it's gone."

He promised to look into it, and I, perhaps naively, believed him.

The next day, during the RWA meeting, the Estate Manager casually mentioned that both the music and the fans in the Lift were indeed working. I stared at him in disbelief.

"Music? Are you sure?" I asked, wondering if I'd somehow gone deaf.

At that moment, the General Secretary, sitting next to me, leaned over with a grin, "Sir, you have a choice - hear the fans of our Schindler lifts or the music - just not both!"

The room erupted in laughter, and I couldn't help but join in. It seemed the lift saga wasn't over just yet. The residents were left with a comical dilemma - cool off in a wind tunnel or ride in peace, serenaded by music.

CHAPTER TWENTY-FOUR

WHEN DOG POOP TURNS INTO A SURVEILLANCE ADVENTURE

In our Society, the dog poop problem had become an epic tale. Frustrated residents, tired of dodging "surprises," pressed the RWA to act. "No pet owner will walk its dog without a poop collector! Social etiquette is the least we expect!" proclaimed the RWA.

While most complied, some 'intellectuals' came up with genius solutions. "Our dog won't poop here. If it does, it'll be in the flower beds!" they announced, certain they'd found a loophole. The RWA wasn't amused. "Nothing doing! Orders are orders," came the curt reply.

Just when we thought the worst was behind us, disaster struck again - the lifts became the new battleground. Poop in the lifts became a recurring horror, with the stench hanging like an unwelcome guest. Furious residents demanded surveillance. "We need cameras in the lifts! Catch the culprits red-handed!"

The RWA was reluctant. "We can't install cameras everywhere, and who's going to watch the footage?" one member asked. "Plus, think of the cost and maintenance!"

Still, under pressure, wireless cameras were installed in the lifts. Without any fancy casing, they worked like a charm. The wide-angle lenses captured everything: the dogs, their owners, and most importantly, the lift floor. Problem solved - or so we thought.

Then someone had to ask, "What if someone steals the cameras? We've lost flower pots, dustbins, even door mats!" Suddenly, what started as a solution to dog poop became a full-blown security crisis. The vendor was summoned to design theft-proof casings. "We need pure steel! Only a narrow slit for the lens," one RWA member insisted, as if somebody was preparing for a heist.

When the vendor arrived with his steel contraption with the tiny camera inside, I couldn't help but question, "Are you sure the camera can still catch the dog?" He assured me, "No worries, sir! It'll capture the entire lift."

But after the installation, the footage was laughable. Courtesy the bulky steel casing not allowing the lens to do its job properly, the camera only recorded pet and its owner's lower halves. The top half of the screen was as useful as a fogged-up mirror.

I burst out laughing. "What are we supposed to do with this? Dog portraits and waist-down shots of owners? How do we catch the real offender?"

"Do we even catch rule-breakers with all these cameras in our Society?" a member asked. "They're just here to make people think twice."

Oddly enough, it worked. The dog poop in the lifts decreased dramatically. We didn't nab any culprits, but in our Society, even a dog poop crisis can morph into a surveillance adventure - where deterrence beats detection any day.

But the adventure isn't over yet - Phase 2 looms on the horizon: figuring out how to capture the dog, its owner, and the lift floor all in the same frame, while the camera remained in its fortress. After all, the security of the gadget was supreme!

CHAPTER TWENTY-FIVE

THE STINKY WALK SAGA : STP, BHAJANS, AND THE 'IRON DOME' OF HOPE

My morning walk took an unexpected turn when I bumped into a resident with a lot on his mind. "This stench is unbearable, especially in the morning," he remarked with a mix of frustration and curiosity. I was more of an evening walker, typically swinging golf clubs during the morning hours. But the recent switch to morning walks gave me a first-hand experience of the nuisance he was talking about.

I was halfway through my first round of our Society when he joined me. Honestly, I prefer walking alone or with my wife, enjoying my thoughts, planning the day, and admiring nature. But this morning wasn't one of those solo saunters. He kept pace with me - a slower one, I might add. Deciding to stay polite, I joined in his conversation.

"Look," I began, responding to his concerns about the awful smell, "the odour comes from the STP - the sewage treatment plant behind our Society. In the morning, when the wind blows eastward, it brings the smell right to us. It's just bad luck for us early walkers."

"That still doesn't tell me what the RWA is doing about it," he pressed on.

So I dived into the whole story. "The STP is virtually defunct - old design, insufficient capacity. We've had several meetings with the developer, Ansals, and the RWS. Initially, they didn't bother listening to us, but after we involved the civil administration, things started moving. They've promised an upgrade, but it's anyone's guess when that will happen. We've all learnt that words can be cheaper than a functioning sewage plant."

He sighed, shaking his head. "So the odour stays until they get to it. God knows when!"

"Pretty much," I said. "But there's also the proposal for a new package-type STP, which should be installed soon... ideally."

He enquired enthusiastically, "It's a package, right? Plug and play, and that's it?"

I couldn't help but grin. "If only it was that easy. It got approved by the RWA recently, but there's a long road ahead - scrutiny of design, tendering, actual execution. The AWHO is supposed to implement it, and it'll easily take more than a year. And don't even get me started on how difficult it was to get the residents on board." I smiled but didn't say anything further.

"Well, at least they agreed. That's something." He seemed to have mellowed a bit, understanding the larger perspective.

As we moved on, approaching the Society temple, he shifted the conversation. "You know, until a month ago, they used to play such beautiful bhajans and kirtans at the temple. It was peaceful - a perfect start to the day. But now they've stopped, and honestly, I think the RWA made a mistake. Why not just lower the volume if people had complaints? Why cut it out completely?" He spoke with visible disappointment.

I hesitated, not wanting to wade into another contentious topic, and secretly wondered how much longer we had left on this lap. That's when he gave me a surprising twist.

"You know, I think the reason we have this unbearable stench now is because those bhajans aren't playing anymore. When they played, there was hardly any odour, and now that they're gone, God seems upset with us!" He spoke with a hint of seriousness, but a glimmer in his eye betrayed a sense of humour.

"So the temple bhajans were our iron dome against the stench?" I smirked, imagining an invisible shield of divine music holding back the awful smells.

"Exactly!" he beamed, nodding. "Who cares about wind directions and old STP designs? Just bring back the bhajans, and let God protect us from this stink!"

We both burst out in amusement, and I couldn't help but appreciate how we had wrapped up our morning walk in such a light-hearted way. Whether it was the temple bhajans, the wind direction, or divine intervention, the conversation had turned an otherwise stinky morning into something genuinely memorable - something to smile and ponder about throughout the day.

CHAPTER TWENTY-SIX

SHAKES AND LAUGHS AFTER A STROLL

It was a cool April evening last year. Winter was fading, but we still needed light woolens to fend off the chill. The Society was full of life, with everyone, even the working-class tenants, back home. It was around 9 PM, and my wife and I were winding down for the night.

We're firm believers in the old adage, "early to bed and early to rise." While the wealth and wisdom part is debatable, I do think it keeps you healthy. After dinner at 8 PM, we always take a leisurely 30-minute stroll around the Society. That evening was no different. After our walk, I settled into bed, with the TV on, and my wife started tidying up the kitchen.

No sooner had I sunk into the pillows when I felt a mild jolt. I shrugged it off. But then, the news flashed on Times Now: "TREMORS FELT ACROSS NORTH INDIA, EPICENTER IN QUETTA!" My brain took a moment to connect the dots. When the fan started shaking wildly and the curtains swayed like a Bollywood dance number, I realized - this was serious.

I shouted, "Earthquake! Earthquake!" and my wife, having felt the tremors too, dashed towards me. We quickly grabbed what we thought were essentials - wallets, ID cards, and credit cards (you know, because financial preparedness is crucial during an earthquake). Without locking the door, we sprinted down seven floors, reaching the ground floor, breathless but determined.

Yet, to our surprise, our neighbours were remarkably calm - some took the elevator down, others just stood near the base of the towers. I was flabbergasted. Had they not heard of basic earthquake safety? We rushed to the open area near the Society gate, urging others to join us.

After 30 minutes of waiting and no further tremors, we decided to head back. On our way, we saw a group of young couples casually standing near the towers. I couldn't resist. "In an earthquake, you don't use the lift! And standing near the buildings? That's dangerous!" I said, feeling quite authoritative. "If you're not going to follow the rules, you might as well stay in your flat!"

One smart young lady, seemingly amused, muttered, "Well, if we stay inside, we could die from both fear and the building collapse. But if we come down and stand here, we'd only die from the collapse. At least that's one less problem!"

I couldn't help but laugh, realizing that even in the face of danger, a little humour could shake off the fear. It was a moment we wouldn't forget - not for the quake itself, but for the unexpected laugh it brought with it.

CHAPTER TWENTY-SEVEN

THE GREAT HORTICULTURE PROMISE : FROM BLUEPRINTS TO PURPLE HEARTS

From the very beginning, our Society's love for greenery was obvious. We wanted a community that felt alive with nature - lush lawns, vibrant flora, and perfectly trimmed hedges. So, with high hopes, we put all our efforts into improving horticulture, even going as far as scrapping an old agency that just wasn't cutting it.

The new agency, however, started strong. They attended to the plants and regularly met with the RWA, giving us confidence in their commitment. So much so, that we found ourselves defending their work whenever any residents complained. Personally, I became emotionally attached to the whole process, spending hours on the ground, chatting with the gardeners, and making suggestions. I even started bonding with the Head Mali and the company's local representative - they appreciated my interest, and together, we were determined to make it work. Of course, there were challenges.

Then came the rainy season that made the grass grow faster than the gardeners could manage, and manpower was stretched thin. We had to constantly nudge the company to improve their staffing and create a real action plan for new plants and further improvements. Eventually, the MD arrived with her entourage and a horticulture expert in tow, promising that all would be fixed. The expert, Mr XYZ, came with high praise, and she seemed to have full confidence in his abilities.

Mr XYZ started by critiquing the Society's appearance - "It looks bad as you enter," he said, making observations that were already obvious to us. He was quick to offer wisdom - "It's not just about manpower, it's about how you use it," and, "We'll fix everything in 15 days." I couldn't help but be impressed by his smooth talk, but I knew better. "Where's the detailed action plan?" I asked.

His answer? "Don't worry, we'll send the blueprint soon."

With a mix of hope and caution, we agreed to give him two more gardeners and 20 days to improve the situation. But I sensed he realized the enormity of the task when his confident tone shifted. Nevertheless, they left, promising the expert would relocate to oversee the improvements.

Days passed with little to show. The promised blueprint was still missing, and the expert was nowhere to be found. After some pressure, we finally got a message from the company - "the blueprint was being worked on," and the expert would arrive the next day.

When he did return, his efforts were minimal - planting a few Purple Hearts near the entrance and scattering Dianella here and there. Even the Head Mali and the local representative seemed unimpressed. Curious, I asked the Head Mali what was going on. He, visibly frustrated, vented, "Sir, we're not fools. I've worked hard to become the Head Mali. These so-called experts come with their degrees, but they lack practical knowledge."

I understood his frustration. "Don't worry," I said, "just keep working hard. You're doing fine job, and we're counting on you."

The local company representative chimed in, "Sir, it's all about teamwork here. On the ground, we have to make it work together - not just the horticulture expert."

And as for that blueprint? Well, we're still waiting. Maybe it'll arrive with the next rainy season.

CHAPTER TWENTY-EIGHT

FROM PARK PANDEMONIUM TO CHAIN-LINK SOLUTIONS : HOW WE FENCED IN THE FUN!

In our Society where retired defence personnel resided, discipline was more than just a way of life - it was a rule. The TMC took their job seriously, ensuring new tenants knew the dos and don'ts of society life.

"This Society is our home, with many disciplined defence personnel. So, no wrongdoings here," declared a senior RWA member of the TMC to a prospective tenant, his stern tone punctuating the air. "Yes, one last thing - no ballgames or cycling in the parks. Children play only in designated areas, no flower plucking, and be mindful of littering!"

With that, the new tenants settled in. But, oh, how quickly they - and their children - forgot the rules. The parks transformed into playgrounds, with kids zooming around on bicycles, parents lounging nearby, enjoying their mischief. Footballs flew, cricket bats swung, and the once-green grass wilted under the chaos.

Complaints piled up. The RWA, now labeled "defunct," was determined to restore order. Security guards were dispatched to monitor the parks, but the task proved tough.

"Sir, bachhe nahin mande. Ajj pher basement da shisha tod ditta hai. Hon tan aale-dwale de vadde bache vi khedan ande hun!" one frustrated guard grumbled. (Translation: "Sir, the children don't listen. Today, they broke another basement ventilator. Now even grown up children come from neighbouring areas to play here!")

Things escalated when a group of residents stormed the RWA office. "How dare you confiscate our child's football? We pay maintenance, and we have a right to use the common areas!" they shouted in unison. One resident, visibly baffled, declared, "If we love green areas so much, let's just paint the ground green!!!!"

The RWA, in a mix of amusement and exasperation, realized that perhaps guards weren't the only solution. And so, one bright member proposed the idea of a "Children's Play Area" enclosed with a chain-link fence. The idea caught on, and soon enough, badminton courts were also added.

When the play area was finally ready, a grand signboard read: "PLAY AREA FOR CHILDREN BELOW 12 YEARS OF AGE." Success, at last! Or so they thought...

One day, the same security guard, now a familiar face, returned with a bemused expression. *"Sir, bacche 12 saal tak haige kiwain pata chaloo?"* he asked. (Translation: "Sir, how do we know if the children are below 12 years old?")

And with that, the RWA burst into laughter, realizing the next challenge had already arrived!

GOLF, GIGGLES AND UNEXPECTED TWISTS : A DAY ON THE GREENS AT PANCHKULA GOLF CLUB

It was one of those picture-perfect mornings when the weather forecast promised a sunny day, and you just knew it was going to be a great outing. We set off from Harbhajan Vihar at 5:45 AM, heading for Panchkula Golf Club, with excitement and lightheartedness in the air. My carpool partner was in a great mood, keeping the ride lively. Even though he was sitting in the co-driver's seat, it was clear he was already in rhythm - his energy was infectious, filling the car with laughter and anticipation.

We expected the drive to take about 50 minutes, but to our surprise, we arrived much earlier than anticipated, with plenty of time before our 7 AM tee-off. The sun was just beginning to rise, casting a golden hue over the course as we prepared to play, courtesy of a reciprocal chit from SEPTA. The fourth golfer in our fourball was a larger-than-life character from DLF Panchkula, full of josh, who loves living life king-size. His quirks were well-known - he couldn't start a game without a cup of tea at the golf course, insisted on perfect playing conditions, and wouldn't hesitate to call it quits mid-game if things didn't go his way.

Today, the course was a dream - no bottlenecks, smooth flow between the fourballs, and ideal conditions to kick off a great game. For the first few holes, the competition was intense, with our opponents keeping us on our toes. However, our friend from DLF seemed a bit off his game, likely because he arrived just in the nick of time and missed his beloved cup of tea! My carpool partner also found himself in a bit of a rough patch, struggling with his short game. But no worries - I managed to carry the team for a while, and the usual lighthearted banter kept the atmosphere fun.

At one point, the conversation turned to the senior citizens' tees, which were placed closer to the ladies' tees. My partner, who had comfortably crossed 60 and was now eligible to play from the senior tees, didn't take kindly to the idea of being lumped together with the ladies. "Sometimes, I hit longer than you guys with my driver, and today, with this 'Percept Lady' golf ball you gifted me, I'm playing even better!" he said proudly, glancing at me. I couldn't help but tease him, "Well then, no extra four strokes for you today!" "In that case," he shot back, "I'll stick to the senior tees!" We all laughed, walking towards the restaurant for a much-needed breakfast after completing the first nine holes.

Refueled and recharged, we headed out to tackle the remaining holes. That's when things started to get really interesting. My partner suddenly found his form, playing brilliantly, while our DLF friend's game began to unravel. It wasn't just the heat of the day - it was the consecutive losses his team suffered over three holes that got to him. His shots went from wayward to downright dangerous, with the ball veering off in all sorts of unexpected directions. We started looking for cover every time he prepared to swing, shouting "Ball" to warn anyone nearby. It became a comical spectacle, with us dodging and waving like we were in a slapstick comedy.

As we approached the 12th hole, our DLF golfer was clearly frustrated and muttered something about possibly withdrawing from the game. I tried to encourage him, saying, "Come on, you're a fighter! Bounce back in these last few holes!" It seemed to work - after a decent tee-off, he stepped up with renewed determination. With all the energy he had left, he shouted "Ball" at the top of his lungs, took a mighty swing with his 3 Wood, and launched the ball... right into my carpool partner.

Now, I'm not saying he hit him on purpose, but the ball took a miraculous 90-degree turn and flew straight into my partner's hand, which, fortunately, was protecting his most vital area. My partner's face was a mix of shock and amusement, more stunned by the ball's trajectory than the actual hit on his little finger. It was one of those moments that reminded me of a Donald Trump story, where a quick reaction saved the day. We couldn't help but laugh, though we made sure to give my partner a moment to shake off the pain.

As the game came to an end, there was a palpable sense of relief. Both my partner and our DLF friend were happy to part ways for a few days, knowing they wouldn't be facing each other on the golf course anytime soon. The day may have been filled with unexpected twists and turns, but it was one for the books - packed with laughter, camaraderie, and the kind of moments that make golf so much more than just a game.

CHAPTER THIRTY

A Meeting Full of Decisions, Drama, and a Dose of Reality

As punctual as always, I reached the office on time. The mood was unmistakably a bit serious, and you could feel it in the room. We waited for a few more members to turn up, though many were already present. The President then commenced the agenda.

As we were settling in, an honourable resident - a well-dressed gentleman, sharp and ready for his office day arrived. We all rose to greet him, one by one, with polite handshakes. After everyone got seated, I wondered if we would continue with our secretive agenda now that an outsider was in the room.

But the visitor wasted no time, and just as the President was getting into the day's agenda, he spoke up. "We find a lot of cabs parked in the basement and even outside. Moreover, many residents' cars lack Parkplus tags. This leads to indiscipline, and it's likely that recent thefts are connected to this lack of order," he said with a lot of concern.

It seemed like he had read the President's notes because he echoed precisely the same concerns the President had begun to express before he arrived. So much for keeping this a secret discussion within the RWA! Realizing there wasn't much of a secret to keep, we continued the discussion.

The big focus was Parkplus tags. The rule was simple - new residents get their tags, cars enter easily. But some residents found one excuse or another to avoid getting them. This led to delays at the gate, unnecessary altercations with security, and no one enjoyed the hassle. Despite repeated reminders to get the tags and the clear benefits they provided, many remained without them.

The meeting gained momentum, with members sharing their concerns. Some blamed the guards for being lax, while others critiqued the residents for disregarding rules. One member suggested, "Let's inspect all residents' cars without tags, tower by tower, and clamp the ones without tags right there." There was support for this plan, with another member adding, "This will send a strong message to the defaulters!"

Listening to the back-and-forth, I grew increasingly unsure if this was the right approach. Finally, I couldn't stay silent any longer. Clearing my throat, I spoke up with a heavy tone, "Don't we secure the border first to prevent infiltration? We don't let infiltrators come in and then deal with them, right? It's basic military strategy." Silence. Some members looked confused, while others seemed intrigued by the analogy.

I explained further, "We need to instruct the security agency clearly. After one week, no residents vehicle without a tag gets in, period. It's the security agency's job to enforce our rules. If they need 'bouncers' to handle unruly residents, they get them. It's better to control the entry rather than create chaos inside." My voice was firm and confident. Slowly, nods of agreement filled the room. No one argued further.

After the usual handshakes and finishing a cup of tea, the honourable visitor left, seemingly satisfied with the outcome.The President then moved on to another very interesting topic I had raised. But that, I suppose, is a story for another day.

Later, at 5:30 sharp, my wife and I went out for our evening walk. We chatted lightly, catching up on each other's day. Feeling proud, I told her about the tough decision we took at the RWA meeting. I thought she'd be impressed until we reached the Community Centre Complex, where she pointed to the LED screen on the wall. It read: "Back-up power and MyGate access will be stopped for all those who don't fix their dripping ACs."

She looked at me slyly and remarked, "Did you ever implement that order? Did the dripping AC problem get solved?"

I felt my pride deflate, sheepish and embarrassed. Bold RWA decisions sounded impressive in meetings, but real implementation? Well, that was an entirely different battle.

CHAPTER THIRTY-ONE

SOLDIER'S REUNION : WHEN TIME, TECHNOLOGY, AND TEA COLLIDE

A few days ago, on a bright morning around 10, my phone buzzed unexpectedly. It was from one of my former youngsters – a bright young officer who had since risen to the prestigious flag rank. He hadn't called for long, nor had he replied to some of my recent messages, so hearing his voice was an unexpected delight.

"Sir, I'd like to come and see you at your house today. What time is convenient for the lady?" he asked.

Overjoyed, I immediately invited him, his wife, and their son, who had accompanied him on a personal trip to Panchkula, for lunch. But he quickly clarified, "No, sir, I'm a bit busy. I'll stop by for tea this evening on my way back to Delhi." All my attempts to persuade him to stay overnight fell flat – his commitments in Delhi the next day were non-negotiable.

My wife and I were thrilled. It had been years since we last saw him. Without missing a beat, she jumped into action, ordering the finest sweets from Amrit Sweets and Paneer Kulcha from Nanak Sweets, preparing for what we affectionately called "high tea." After all, the officer had once served with me – he was a thorough professional, a brilliant sportsman, and a steadfast soldier who always held his head high, even in front of his superiors. He never missed wishing me on Teacher's Day and always regarded me as a mentor. His wife, a warm and caring lady, shared a close bond with my wife, often seeking advice on matters related to the welfare of the regiment's ladies during her husband's command days.

By 4 in the evening, my wife and I were dressed to impress. We knew our guests well – they were always punctual, if not early. My subaltern's soldierly discipline dictated that 4:00 PM meant arriving at 3:55 PM sharp. So, dressed in my finest trousers and bushirt, and my wife in her semi formal attire, we were ready to welcome them. The dining table was set, drinks were prepared, and the soft melody of old Hindi songs from the 1960s filled the air. Even the Society's gatekeeper had been informed in advance for their smooth entry. We stood ready, anticipating their arrival.

But then, 4:00 PM came and went. So did 4:15, and then 4:30. No sign of them. I started to worry – no call, and my attempts to reach them went unanswered. I was puzzled. How could this disciplined couple have changed so much? I had sent them my exact address, even asking them to call once they were nearby. Something wasn't right.

Just as I was lost in thoughts, the doorbell rang. Expecting our evening maid, I casually opened the door, only to be greeted by my officer, his wife, and their 29-year-old special child. My emotions were a mix of surprise and joy as I welcomed them in.

After warm hugs and pleasantries, we settled into our cozy drawing room. Soon, the refreshments followed.

"Sir," he began, "I must apologize for being out of touch for so long. I knew about your illness and wanted to come by personally to check on you. Even with today's busy schedule, I couldn't leave without meeting you. But let's not dwell on what happened to such a fit officer like you. We're just glad to see you doing well." His words, filled with sincerity, brought a sense of relief.

The ladies, meanwhile, dove into animated conversation, exchanging news, tips, and even the address of a famous shoe maker in Ambala Cantt – a recommendation that my wife later shared with half the ladies in our Society.

I couldn't resist teasing my young officer about their delayed arrival and his unresponsiveness to my calls. What followed was a story that had us all in stitches.

"Sir," he began, "I put my faith in Google Maps – the 'Google aunty,' as we call her. I set the location you sent, and we left Panchkula confident we'd reach in 55 minutes. It was 2:50 PM, so we were sure to be on time. I didn't call, thinking you'd be enjoying your famous afternoon nap! Everything went smoothly until we reached Landran Chowk. Google aunty instructed us to turn right, and then again near Rai Farm, she said left. We obediently followed, until I realized something was wrong around 4. No signal, no calls. Nothing."

He paused for dramatic effect before continuing. "I thought you might've built yourself a grand villa in a village, sir! We ended up in Kailon village, navigating narrow lanes blocked by tractor trolleys, convinced you had chosen a rural retreat!"

It was a comedy of errors, all thanks to Google. They had missed the main entry to our Society and ended up on a scenic detour instead.

As I laughed, I reminded him of the dangers of blindly trusting technology. He sheepishly agreed, and the evening ended with laughter, warm memories, and promises to stay in better touch.

That day, we didn't just share tea and snacks – we shared stories, struggles, and the unshakable bonds of friendship that no amount of time or distance could diminish.

CHAPTER THIRTY-TWO

THE ZOO CHRONICLES OF OUR SOCIETY

The residents of our Society had grown weary. The latest theft in the basement - the battery of a car mysteriously gone missing - had sparked a storm on the Society's WhatsApp Group. Messages poured in like a monsoon, each one carrying a fresh complaint.

"Petrol was siphoned from my bike!" typed one resident.

"Carpet kept in a box was stolen from my parking slot!" added another.

The chat became a chaotic mix of anger and frustration, each new notification a reminder that our Society was seemingly turning into a crowded local market, rife with petty theft.

The RWA had tried everything. Just a month ago, when a motorbike battery had gone missing, they had swung into action like detectives in a crime thriller. They grilled the security agency, analyzed every possible loophole, and eventually caught the culprit - a tenant from the Society itself. Another time, a garbage collector was caught with stolen goods and promptly handed over to the local police. Measures were taken, guards were reshuffled, patrolling intensified, and for a while, everything seemed calm.

But calm is just the pause before the next storm.

The WhatsApp Group, now reignited with fresh thefts, turned into a digital brainstorming session. Ideas flowed freely - some amusing, some somewhat reasonable.

"Make the security staff pay for any losses!" suggested an annoyed resident.

"RWA should compensate for the stolen goods!" demanded another.

"Close half the gates and put those guards in the basement!" someone proposed.

And then, the chuckle of the suggestions appeared.

One resident declared, "Since the parking slot is my property, why don't I just put up a grill around it - or better yet, a shutter to enclose it."

At first, it seemed like a joke - a desperate attempt at sarcasm to lighten the mood. But no, it gained traction, and soon enough, people were genuinely discussing gated, shuttered parking slots.

The image in my mind was vivid and amusing: a basement filled with individual cages, each car behind its own bars like exotic animals on display. Was this our Society or a zoo for inanimate objects? The thought left me half-amused, half-horrified.

Are we really so afraid of losing our possessions that we'd rather live in a zoo-like community than cooperate to find a real solution? Are we ready to exchange our openness for metal bars and shutters, all because of petty theft?

Instead of helping the RWA find a practical solution, many residents preferred to blame, criticize, and suggest makeshift fixes that made our Society look less like a community and more like a poorly constructed fortress. It was clear - everyone wanted someone else to take responsibility.

But maybe, what we need isn't another grill or another guard, but a change in mindset. Within available maintenance funds, beefing up the much-needed security staff isn't feasible, but the RWA's plea was simple: let's be watchful and responsible, together.

CHAPTER THIRTY-THREE

WHEN ADMIRATION TURNS DEADLY - THE TALE OF THE OVER-PRAISED SNAKE PLANT

Not very long ago, an old coursemate, despite being from a different arm, called to say he and two of his college friends would be dropping by. I was still recovering from a bad spell of sickness, and visits from well-wishers had become the norm. The last time we'd met was at another course mate's son's wedding in Mandi, so I was eager to see him again.

Naturally, I informed my wife, who immediately sprang into action, preparing for the guests. Zomato got us some goodies from Amrit Sweets in 3B2 market, and I set up the bar, anticipating a relaxed evening.

Around 5 PM, the MyGate App buzzed, seeking my approval for a cab carrying three male passengers. No surprises there - it was them. I quickly made my way downstairs to receive them. As the cab approached, my friend waved enthusiastically, and before they could even step out properly, he gave me a hearty hug. After the introduction, I learnt that both his friends weren't just any college mates - they were ex-Ranji cricket players, and one out of them had played for India. As a cricket lover, I vaguely remembered their faces.

We took the lift up to our seventh-floor flat. My wife welcomed them warmly. As we were about to enter, one of my friend's mates paused to remove his shoes. "We don't enter homes with shoes on," he explained briefly. We respected his tradition.

Settling in, I asked the customary question: "What's the poison for you guys?" My coursemate smiled, "Thanks, but we have a flight back to Pune tonight, so just a hot cup of coffee will do." The others nodded, and soon enough, coffee and snacks were served. They were appreciative, and my wife beamed.

While we chatted, the friend who had removed his shoes noticed a painting in the living room. "I've seen something like this in a Florida mall recently - it's quite expensive! Where did you get it?" he asked. My wife, always eager to share, proudly replied, "Oh, this is from Lahaul-Spiti. It's drawn on a raw palm leaf using charcoal, and it was gifted to my husband when he was Chief Engineer visiting the area. The local MLA then said it's highly exported." The admiration in the room was palpable.

The other friend admired our indoor greenery. He walked over to the snake plant, touched it, and remarked, "This snake plant is so lush! You've got a green thumb, Ma'am." Pleased, my wife offered him an extra helping of snacks.

After about two hours, they thanked us for our hospitality and bid farewell, with repeated mentions of the beautiful snake plant. My coursemate was happy to see me recovering.

Later, in our good mood, my wife asked me to move the snake plant to the balcony for its usual sunlight rotation. But that night, a heavy storm hit. We felt it while sleeping but had no idea about the chaos it caused.

Morning revealed the damage: the ceramic pots were shattered, and our beloved snake plants were strewn across the balcony floor. After a miserable breakfast, we rushed to buy new ceramic pots and tried to propagate what was left of our once-mighty snake plant.

Later, my coursemate messaged from Pune: "Thanks, Kats, for the wonderful evening and your great hospitality. My friends couldn't stop talking about your lovely snake plant all the way." I replied, "Thank you so much for coming by - it was such fun! Oh, by the way, that snake plant your friend admired? I guess it just couldn't handle all that extra attention and praise! Next time, we'll pick a sturdier favourite!"

Now, each time we look at the propagated bits of our snake plant, we can't help but chuckle at how even plants can buckle under pressure.

CHAPTER THIRTY-FOUR

FROM CLAMPED CARS TO CANADIAN DREAMS : THE ENIGMA OF MY MULTITALENTED NEIGHBOUR

It was an ordinary day as I made my way to the RWA office for a crucial meeting. Before I could reach, our Society Security Supervisor caught me, looking a bit stressed.

"*Sir, tuhanu pata hai ae Chinese car kidi hai? Aidi roj complaint aa rahi hai, kadi aethe kadi uthe park kiti hondi hai. Society da Parkplus tag vi nahi hai,*" he said in his usual hurried tone. (Translation - "Sir, any idea who this Chinese car belongs to? We are getting complaints daily about it being parked in other residents' slots. It doesn't even have our Society Park Plus tag.")

Then he added, "*General Secretary da hukam hai ki clamp karo is car nu,*" meaning the General Secretary had ordered him to clamp the car.

I shrugged, having no clue about the car's owner. "I have no idea about it. Do whatever has been ordered," I replied, brushing it aside, as I headed to the office.

The meeting was crucial, discussing the road construction project outside our Society in collaboration with the RWS of Ansals. Naturally, most of the RWA members, along with the President, were present.

But twice during the meeting, the Security Supervisor tried to intervene, clearly troubled by something. We asked him to wait outside until we finished. After nearly two hours, when the meeting finally concluded, we let him in.

Trailing behind him was a young man with a slender frame, wild hair, and a long untidy beard. Dressed casually in black clothes and slippers, he looked upset, to say the least.

Without any pleasantries, he burst out, *"Mujhe pareshan kiya ja raha hai. Main is Society mein apne parents aur family ke saath aram se rahta hoon. Meri car clamp kar di hai. Mujhe kahin jaldi jana tha. Ye kya majak hai!"* He was livid. (Translation : "I'm being unnecessarily harassed. I live in this Society peacefully with my parents. My car has been clamped, and I had somewhere important to go. What kind of joke is this?"

The Security Supervisor calmly explained the issue to the RWA members. This guy had been parking his car wherever he wanted without a valid Parkplus tag. He had been warned multiple times, but nothing changed. Eventually, the RWA decided he had to pay the fine to get his car de-clamped and acquire the parking tag that same day. The young man, fuming, reluctantly paid the fine and left. The Supervisor followed soon after.

For a few days, things were quiet - until, of course, the same car appeared again, parked haphazardly, still without the tag. More warnings were given, but endless excuses followed. Finally, the RWA took drastic action and denied the car entry altogether. After that, the car vanished. Was it a case of a stolen car being brought for safe heaven inside? Who knows!

Meanwhile, my wife had her own complaints. She had noticed pizza boxes, empty beer cans, and other trash strewn on our floor corridor at irregular hours almost everyday. She wasn't happy about it, but I dismissed it, suggesting she ask the tower maid to clean it up. Little did I know, there was a bigger connection to all this.

One morning, as my wife and I were heading out, locking up our flat, we encountered the same eccentric guy. This time, though, he greeted us with a broad smile."Good morning, sir! I'm your neighbour. I saw you that day with the RWA," he said enthusiastically.

Shocked and curious, I asked him what he did for a living. His reply, however, caught me off guard. "Sir, I'm a freelancer. I do many things - compose Punjabi songs, sing them, and shoot videos. My YouTube channel is quite popular," he said, proudly.

Before I could process it all, he broke into an impromptu performance, awkwardly shaking his body as he sang a few lines from his latest song. It wasn't exactly my taste, but I nodded politely, encouraging him before making a quick exit.

A few days later, when my daughter and her husband visited us, I couldn't resist telling them the whole story - how our quirky neighbour had his car clamped, his outburst, and his unexpected revelation about being a YouTube star. My son-in-law, curious as ever, pulled up his YouTube channel. What he found left us all astonished.

"Papa, this guy has lakhs of followers, I must meet him to get a few lessons!" he exclaimed. The pieces were falling into place. This wasn't just some random guy; he was a rising folk singer. Suddenly, the frequent appearance of expensive food packages outside his door made sense.

Curiosity got the better of me, so I decided to visit his flat and invite him over to meet my family. His wife opened the door and, when I asked for him, said, "Oh, he's not here. He's gone to Chandigarh to drop off a passenger in his cab. He'll be back late tonight."

Wait- what? A famous YouTuber was moonlighting as a cab driver? I walked back home, my surprise growing with every step. When I told my family, it only added more fuel to their curiosity. My son-in-law, ever the skeptic, remarked, "Papa, don't take this guy lightly. He's probably making a fortune."

But something still didn't add up. If he was making that much money, why was he involved in all these notorious activities, and... cab driving business?

Just when I thought the story couldn't get any stranger, a final twist came my way.

A few days later, my carpool buddy, a veteran like me, was upset about being denied a visa to Canada. He had always been a respectable, decent man. Yet here he was, frustrated by bureaucracy.

That evening, guess who I ran into? Yes, my eccentric neighbour, now sporting a completely new look - trimmed beard, neat mushroom haircut. I almost didn't recognize him.

"How are you? What's with this new look?" I asked, trying to hide my disbelief.

His reply floored me: *"Meri nayi album ban rahi hai. Uske liye new look banaya hai. 10-15 dino mein Canada ja raha hoon shoot ke liye."* (Translation : "I'm shooting a new album. This new look is for that. I'm heading to Canada in 10-15 days for the shoot.")

Wait, what?!! This guy, who couldn't manage to park his car properly and can't even stand straight had easily secured a Canadian visa to shoot a music video, while my distinguished friend couldn't get one for a simple visit?

As I sit back and think about it all, I can't help but laugh at how strange life can be. Who would've thought I'd be living next door to a clamped-car-driving, folk-singing, cab-driving, YouTube star heading off to Canada?

SWING IN THE DARK : WHEN GOLF MEETS PUZZLE

It was a quiet evening, just before dusk, when my phone buzzed. "Hi Kats! How's life? Do you know Colonel PQR posted in Andaman? He's a Sapper officer." The voice on the other end was familiar yet elusive, and before I could even respond, came another question: "I'm planning a holiday trip to Andaman in November and need some help."

Now, who the hell on earth knows my nickname, my profession, and calls me out of the blue for travel advice? My mind raced to solve this mini-mystery. It had to be the flat owner from our tower, whom I'd met briefly six months ago while riding the escalator with my wife. A well-built fellow with a booming voice, he was in such a rush back then that I could barely recall the conversation.

"I've retired now and don't know this Colonel PQR," I replied, trying to catch up with the unexpected chat. "But you shouldn't have any trouble in Port Blair; they're a helpful bunch there."

Our conversation then shifted to his house construction project in Himachal Pradesh. Intrigued, I asked, "So, where are you planning to settle down, considering you have a flat here too?"

He answered in Hindi - *"Basoon ga wahan, rahoon ga yahan"*, which loosely translates to "I'll settle there but stay here." Completely puzzled, I asked for clarification. Instead of an explanation, he dodged with, "Leave it, partner. I'll explain some other day. How's your golf going?"

Relieved to be on a more familiar topic, I told him about my recent round of 18 holes with some fellow Society golfers. "I'm in!" he exclaimed, thrilled at the thought of joining us. I filled him in on our weekly rounds, mentioning Panchkula Golf Club for the upcoming Friday.

Then, he threw a curveball - "I'll first brush up my golfing skills at Bestech Mall."

"Bestech Mall?" I laughed. "There's no golf range there!"

Without missing a beat, he wrapped up with, "I'll explain it all over a drink tomorrow once we meet in your flat".

After hanging up, I sat there staring at my phone, utterly perplexed. Basoon ga wahan, rahoon ga yahan? Practice golf at a mall? His cryptic remarks kept replaying in my head. Was this flat owner planning some secret relocation with hidden golf training at a mall, or had I just been drawn into the world's most bizarre sense of humour?

Finally, it was my wife who cracked the code with a knowing smile. "Relax," she said, "Some people start their evening drinks well before dusk. Don't stress too much! *'Basoon ga wahan, rahoon ga yahan'* likely means he'll settle in Himachal but keep visiting here. And when he mentioned practicing at Bestech Mall, he probably meant Beverley Golf Range, which is just a few kilometers away."

I laughed, realizing she was probably right. There were no secret plans or hidden golf courses. It was just another swing in the dark, where golf met puzzle - and I was simply overthinking, or in golfing terms, over par.

CHAPTER THIRTY-SIX

THE CURIOUS CASE OF THE ONE-EARED EARRING

Every once in a while, the quirky fashion trends of youngsters in our Society catch my eye. Lately, it's been a particular group of boys with half-mushroom haircuts, hands stuffed in their pockets, strutting around in flashy shorts, t-shirts, and the ubiquitous flip-flops. They don't just walk - they ride bikes, often as triple riders, and of course, none of them wear helmets. And there was one more thing - ear pins, but only in one ear! Their entire getup was a sight to behold. I couldn't help but wonder - what's with that single ear pin? Was there a hidden secret behind it?

It wasn't long before the ear pin trend was replaced by something even more dramatic - earrings! But not just any earrings. These were special; flat-bottomed, gold ones. Now this was becoming a serious fashion mystery. Naturally, this odd transformation became the talk of the town at the RWA office. Some suggested these rural youngsters once wore silver anklets, and over time, that evolved into ear pins and eventually these earrings. The why, though? No one seemed to know, but everyone had a joke about it.

Well, nosiness was eating me alive.

It so happened that I was due for my monthly haircut. Now, let me tell you, missing my haircut schedule throws me off completely! Luckily, we have a salon right within our Society called Master Cutz - clean, professional, and always packed. I called ahead and snagged a 5 PM appointment. When I arrived, I was a bit disappointed to find out my usual barber was on leave. Instead, a young lad with all the same trendy attributes (including that one-ear earring) was there to give me my trim.

Reluctantly, I sat in the chair after a refreshing shampoo wash. The boy seemed skilled and friendly, so I eased up. As I stared in the mirror, I couldn't stop focusing on his shiny earring. Curiosity got the better of me, and as we casually chatted about his name, training, and family, I finally popped the question that had been haunting me for weeks.

"Ye aap ladke ek kaan mein wali kyon pahnte ho? Maine pahle ladkon ko koka pahne dekha tha." (Translation: "Why do you boys wear one earring? I used to see just ear pins before.")

Without much thinking, he confidently replied, *"Ae ji sehat lai changa honda hai. Buri nazar to vi bachwanda hai."* (Translation: "Oh, it's good for health and protects us from the evil eye.")

I had to stop myself from bursting into laughter. So, this mysterious earring was a health booster and a charm against evil! If that were true, I wondered why not wear earrings in both ears for double the protection? I chuckled as he finished the haircut, paid via the barcode, and walked out, feeling both enlightened and amused.

As I strolled out, still mulling over the boy's "scientific" answer, I thought to myself - could it be that the ear pin was a kind of Mk I health shield and now, the earring was an upgraded Mk II, offering more comprehensive coverage against ailments? I was still laughing inside when I bumped into my wife during her evening walk.

Unable to resist, I narrated the entire saga to her. She's always in the know about Society's latest trends, so I asked, "Do you really think the ear pin and earring could be for health and warding off evil?"

She didn't miss a beat. With a smirk, she said, "Good health to deal with those bouncers RWA brought in to control unruly residents, and protection from the TMC's evil eye, since they're known to grill newcomers!"

I couldn't stop laughing. The mystery of the earring was finally solved - or so it seemed!

THE MYSTERY OF THE UNCLAIMED VEHICLES AND THE SECURITY SUPERVISOR'S WOES

"AB Singh, ajj kiven ethe ana hoya?" I asked the Security Supervisor, who was standing outside the RWA office, waiting to meet the Vice President. ("AB Singh, what gets you here today?")

"Sir, kuch lawaris gadian di report deni si," he replied with a sigh. ("I was asked to give a report about some unclaimed vehicles.")

The problem had been brewing for a while - unclaimed vehicles were sitting untouched in our Society, parked in places they shouldn't be. A scooter here, a car there, parked in unauthorized slots or even in somebody else's space. Guest parking slots, meant for visitors, were being occupied by these mysterious vehicles, causing frustration for residents and their guests. It was high time to sort it all out.

Mr AB Singh was given the task of identifying all these vehicles, using resident records to compile a thorough report. And, did he deliver - a list of around 25 unclaimed vehicles! The RWA jumped at the sight of the numbers. It was time for action.

Multiple requests were sent to residents - emails, WhatsApp messages, and alerts on MyGate - asking them to claim and move their vehicles. Threats of fines were made, but there was no response. It seemed like no one cared. So, the RWA decided to take the next step - clamp those vehicles.

It was quite the sight: AB Singh and one of the guards wandering around, clamping wheels, one vehicle at a time. The residents watched on with a mix of amusement and satisfaction - finally, something was being done!

Yet, days passed, and still, nothing happened. Nobody came to the office to de-clamp their vehicle. Not a soul admitted ownership. It was puzzling. How could there be so many unclaimed vehicles in our Society? And then darker thoughts crossed our minds - could there be a gang operating within, dealing in stolen vehicles?

Eventually, we turned to the local police. We requested them to take away these unclaimed vehicles. But dealing with the police is never easy - they quizzed with several questions, often looking at us like we were the suspects. After a lot of back and forth, the police refused. Defeated, we decided to park all the unclaimed vehicles in one central location in the basement and left it at that.

Then, a new wave of trouble hit us - petty thefts. A motorbike's battery disappeared one day, petrol was siphoned from a scooter the next, and even coolers vanished from the basement parking. Each incident seemed random, but it was enough to shake everyone up. The RWA held meeting after meeting, discussing with the security agency and brainstorming among ourselves to find ways to stop it. Almost daily, AB Singh and his team would be called in for questioning, looking more dejected each time.

We did eventually have some success. We caught one of the tenants involved in a theft, and on another occasion, it turned out to be the garbage collector. Things seemed to calm down for a while, but then another incident - the battery of a car was stolen. The residents were livid. The security supervisor was summoned again, every single day.

One day, I saw the Security Supervisor standing outside the office, his face longer than ever. I couldn't help but ask, *"AB Singh, aina udas kyon ho? Tusi te bade husmukh hon."* (Translation: "AB Singh, why are you so sad today? You are such a cheerful person.")

His reply caught me off guard. *"Sadi te roj kutte-khae ho rahi hai. Samaj nahi anda ae chor lawaris gadian di chijan kyon nahi churande?"* ("We are ridiculed every day. But I wonder why the thieves don't steal from the unclaimed vehicles instead?")

I laughed, but his words lingered in my mind. How strange it was that, despite everything being stolen - from petrol to batteries - these unclaimed vehicles remained untouched. It was almost as if they were invisible to the thieves, immune to the mischief. Perhaps there was something about these vehicles, some untold story, that made them different. And maybe that story was the key to understanding the chaos around us.

CHAPTER THIRTY-EIGHT

THE LEAK THAT KEEPS ON LEAKING : OUR VERY OWN WATER PARK!

"Why are all the lawns dug up so badly?" I asked, more confused than upset, as my wife and I surveyed the mess. What should have been a pristine garden now looked like a battlefield, with trenches, piles of mud, and debris scattered everywhere.

"I thought construction was over years ago," my wife added, equally puzzled. We had just moved in, excited about the green spaces, but instead, we were greeted by what looked like the aftermath of a large-scale excavation.

It didn't take long to find out why. The PD, sent by AWHO to oversee the work, explained when I met him. "The basement's leaking," he said, matter-of-factly. "The original contractor is handling the repairs - it'll be fixed in about a month."

I raised an eyebrow. "But the Society is only a few years old, and flats are still being handed over. Isn't this a little too soon for such problems?"

He shifted in his seat. "Well, sir... the previous PDs might know more, but I'll make sure it's sorted out this time." His confident smile didn't reassure me much, but I hoped for the best.

Weeks turned into months. The lawns remained a mess, and residents grew increasingly restless. Then, after nearly five months, we got the news: the basement was finally fixed. Relief washed over us - until the monsoon rains arrived.

What followed was pure chaos. Instead of being repaired, the basement became a disaster zone. Water streamed in from every direction: walls, roof - you name it. Fountains sprang from cracks, and the ceiling drizzled water like it had been designed that way. We didn't have a leak; we had our very own indoor water park!

The RWA sent a letter to AWHO, pointing out the spectacular failure. AWHO responded with a formal note, announcing that Asian Paints, known for fixing leakage and seepage, would take over the repairs. Six months, they promised, and the issue would be resolved.

The digging began - again. More trenches crisscrossed the lawns, making the place look like a war zone. But this time, the workers seemed more efficient, injecting cement slurry into the walls to waterproof the basement, using a technique called Pressure Grouting.

Just when we started to feel hopeful, the rainy season transformed the trenches into something resembling the canals of Amsterdam. Instead of gondolas, though, we had stagnant water, with mosquitoes multiplying at an alarming rate. It was a strange mix of comedy and frustration as we watched our lawns turn into a breeding ground for pests.

Eventually, even that problem seemed under control - until the next twist. "Kids have been throwing stones into the channels, damaging the waterproof taping," the PD reported. Apparently, this was the latest reason for delays. By now, it felt like we were trapped in a never-ending loop, where each solution sparked a new problem - like trying to plug leaks in a sinking ship.

To add to the absurdity, the PD threatened the RWA about raising a claim against it, accusing us of damaging the taping after we sent a letter about the removal of brick cladding from the basement walls. Their explanation? "The cladding was just decorative. It's not necessary for the structure."

"Then why have it in the first place?" the RWA quizzed.

Ironically, the taping wasn't damaged when the concrete was poured over it - though apparently stones caused more harm than mass concreting work. As repairs dragged on and deadlines slipped by, we couldn't help but wonder: Will the basement leak again? And if it does, who will be blamed this time?

For now, we wait, hoping the next downpour won't bring more broken promises and watery chaos. But if it does, we'll know we've simply been part of a long-running comedy, with the leak playing the starring role.

CHAPTER THIRTY-NINE

THE RFID RIDDLE : THE CASE OF THE MISSING CARS

It was an unusually quiet evening walk, almost too quiet. My wife, ever the sharp observer, noticed right away. "I hardly see any vehicles in the guests' parking slots. Even in the basement, fewer bikes and cars are parked," she said, her voice full of suspicion.

"Maybe it's the long Dussehra weekend," I suggested, distracted by a phone call from a friend confirming Sunday's reception venue. But she wasn't convinced.

"Long weekends have come and gone, but I've never seen the parking this empty," she insisted, clearly curious. I, of course, decided to let her wonder a little longer, silently enjoying the mystery.

We kept walking, her curiosity growing by the minute. As we neared the main gate, things took an odd turn. Outside, a convoy of cars waited, their owners anxiously shuffling through papers. An office guy sat behind a table, surrounded by a pile of documents and dealing with a queue of residents.

"It's the Parkplus RFID tag rush," said AB Singh, the security supervisor, catching my wife's puzzled look. "No tag, no entry for residents' vehicles."

That was it! The RFID rule was finally being enforced. My wife had heard about it in the Society WhatsApp Group. After a few petty thefts, the RWA had upped the security measures. Residents needed RFID tags to enter, while visitors just had to sign in. But why the sudden drop in parked cars?

"Why, though?" she asked again, clearly puzzled. I, of course, kept dodging the answer for fun.

The next day, at the RWA meeting, the RFID tags dominated the conversation. Some praised the tighter security; others whined about the inconvenience. I couldn't help but point out, "First, people complained about lax security, and now they're upset about it being too strict. The RWA is everyone's favourite punching bag!" The members laughed in agreement, nodding along.

Later that evening, during our walk, I finally gave in and explained the disappearing cars. Many residents had blatantly violated the society rules, parking more vehicles than their allotted spaces. They'd been sneaking their extra cars into the guests' parking. But with the RFID rule now being enforced, those untagged, extra cars were left outside. Hence, the mysteriously empty lots.

I proudly credited the RWA for enforcing the rule. "Now that's how you get the things done! The President will surely secure his second term.

My wife grinned as we approached the gate. "Did you see those two burly guys in black safari suit? I think the real reason everyone's obeying the rules is the presence of those bouncers, not your RWA's bold decision."

She was right, of course. I had to admit – sometimes, the simplest solution involves a bit of muscle.

CHAPTER FORTY

THE PAVING PARADOX OF OUR SOCIETY

The AGBM was in full swing, and the atmosphere was electric with anticipation. Residents eagerly awaited the budget presentation, a harbinger of the projects planned for the forthcoming year. As the projected list illuminated the screen, a collective gasp echoed through the room. There it was, prominently displayed – the repair of the internal road within our Society.

The excitement was palpable. Glances were exchanged, and murmurs of approval reverberated throughout the audience. After all, they had longed for this moment. The promise of a newly paved road heralded not only convenience but also the potential elevation of the Society's prestige. Yet, the crux of the matter was this: would it be a bituminous surface or a paver block construction?

Thus commenced an impromptu debate.

"I've observed that bituminous roads offer unparalleled smoothness and superior drainage," proclaimed one resident, clearly positioning himself as a road aficionado.

"While that may be true," countered another from the middle row, "paver blocks last longer and are easier to maintain. Plus, no potholes!"

The discussion escalated into a fervent exchange of opinions. Sensing the need for intervention, I interjected with a smile, articulating the merits and drawbacks of both alternatives. Finally, we reached a consensus: "Why not a hybrid construction? Primarily bituminous with select paver blocks." The room nodded in agreement, and with that, the happiness quotient soared.

However, as is often the case, the road to progress was fraught with complications.

Some RWA members, in their infinite wisdom, suggested postponing the project for six months. "Why delay?" I was perplexed as I knew the residents were eager for swift action; they had been vocal in their enthusiasm. Every other day during my evening walk, I encountered a resident brimming with excitement. "When will the road be completed?" they would ask, eyes gleaming with anticipation. I'd respond with an encouraging grin, but even I was beginning to grow impatient.

After a month of deliberation, the RWA finally resolved to expedite the project. Although we had squandered precious time, the momentum was now building.

As anticipation within the RWA mounted, discussions grew increasingly animated. "The road must be impeccably smooth!" insisted one member during a meeting. "Will we have proper markings on the sides?" another inquired, while yet another enthusiastically suggested, "Don't forget those shiny inserts in the middle; they look spectacular!" I said you mean those cat eyes!

With each meeting, the road became the focal point of our discussions. "The paver blocks must align flawlessly with the bituminous sections!" one member asserted. It felt as though we were preparing for the arrival of a royal heir rather than a simple road repair.

Meanwhile, during my evening strolls, residents were more than willing to share their feedback. "You know, the existing paver block surface is sinking at places; water collects there and becomes a hazard!" remarked one frequent walker. Another added, "The manhole covers are dangerous! Someone is bound to trip if we don't address that."

I found myself inundated with observations, yet I relished the enthusiasm. This was a road everyone was passionate about.

Eventually, the Estate Manager presented the draft tender for review. I gently studied, ensuring all essential details were included, and with a few prudent adjustments, we were ready to float the tender enquiry.

The day of the tender opening arrived, and we awaited the bids with bated breath. To our astonishment, only one tender was submitted. Just one! We had no choice but to extend the date to solicit broader participation.

When the revised tenders finally came in, yet another twist awaited us – the quotes varied dramatically. Something was amiss. "I suspect they didn't fully comprehend the accounting units in the tender," I noted. The RWA decided to meet with the vendors for clarification, and lo and behold, some had misinterpreted the specifications. After providing the necessary guidance, we requested revised quotes.

Now, as we await those new bids, all eyes are on the weather gods. I am glued to AccuWeather, fervently hoping the temperature remains above 30 degrees Celsius. Why? Because we cannot compromise on the quality of this road. It's not merely a construction project; it's a testament to the residents' faith in their RWA.

As I gaze at the shifting clouds, I can't help but chuckle. Building a road has morphed into quite the epic saga. Let's see what lies ahead on this winding journey...

A Ride through Reflection, Ego, and a Little Army Wit!

It was one of those casual afternoons when life throws you a pleasant curveball. My neighbour, a man of great wit and someone I hold dear - especially after he's saved my life on more than one occasion - called out, "I believe you've been invited to the wedding reception tonight? Why don't we go together? My wife and I are heading there too."

"Absolutely, sir! It'd be my pleasure to drive you both. My wife will enjoy catching up with Ma'am too," I responded, delighted at the thought of sharing the evening.

In true soldierly fashion, I arrived at his tower at 6:20 PM - ten minutes ahead of schedule in my freshly cleaned Skoda Kushaq. We didn't wait for long before my neighbour and his wife emerged, but when they did, it was worth the wait.

There he was, looking dapper in his signature turban, a stylish half-sleeve jacket, and a scarf draped around his neck. His wife, a vision of elegance in a traditional Zari plazo suit, radiated grace. As I glanced down at my own light-coloured trousers and dark full-sleeve shirt, I momentarily felt underdressed but reminded myself it's the company that counts, not the clothes.

The journey began smoothly, and as we maneuvered through the inevitable traffic jams of city life, the conversation flowed naturally. The ladies in the back caught up on all things - sharing updates on their children's latest accomplishments and the avalanche of wedding-season sweets they couldn't seem to escape. Meanwhile, the gentlemen - myself included talked shop about our Society, particularly the increasing grumbles from residents over the stricter entry rules. Between the banter, the radio hummed in the background, adding to the charm of the drive.

Just as we approached a gas station, I suddenly remembered, "I need to top up the petrol." The attendant motioned to open the petrol lid. I tried, but nothing happened. I pressed the button again, and still, no luck. That's when it dawned on me - my overzealous cleaning spree before we left had disturbed the settings. After a moment of adjusting, the issue was fixed, and we were back on the road.

By the time we pulled up to the Gymkhana Club at 8 PM, we were fashionably late. The reception area was a delightful sight - an open-air pandal adorned with twinkling lights and an excited crowd already deep into the celebration. After a warm greeting from the host and his wife, we moved further inside.

"It's a small world," I remarked as I spotted several familiar faces. The crowd was almost entirely from the army circle, each guest having some connection to the host. After some time, my neighbour and I split up, joining our own sets of friends. One of the first faces I recognized was my old carpool partner, dressed in his brand new sharp black suit, sans wife. "Perhaps the absence is to enjoy the drinks a bit more freely," I chuckled to myself.

As the night unfolded, the air was filled with stories from the past, hearty laughter, and the smooth rhythms of a jazz band. Drinks flowed generously, and the appetizers seemed never-ending. The atmosphere took me back to the parties of our army days - full of life, where camaraderie was the main dish, and ego was left at the door.

But as I mingled, I couldn't help but notice the stark contrast between the guests. Some were fully immersed in the revelry, laughing loudly, clinking glasses, and dancing to the music. They had clearly embraced their post-retirement lives with joy and contentment. Others, however, seemed somewhat detached - even hesitant to move to the bar to recharge their glasses, barely interacting, as if waiting for happiness to come find them rather than seeking it out.

I ran into an old acquaintance from our CME days. "Sir, what a pleasure to see you after three decades!" I exclaimed. "You look just as dashing as back in the day!" He stood there, in his classic model-like pose - one leg slightly bent, one hand in his pocket, and the other gesturing elegantly, reminding me of those Raymond ads we used to joke about. "Old habits die hard, don't they?" I quipped, and we both shared a hearty laugh.

I then found myself speaking with another senior veteran, now working in disaster management. His demeanour was more serious, his energy subdued. "What keeps you busy these days, sir?" I asked. He sighed and looked away, clearly disenchanted with the life he was now leading. "Not much," he replied, and I realized the weight of dissatisfaction he was carrying.

There were others like him - guests who seemed burdened by their past glories, as if they hadn't yet accepted that life had moved on. One man, a retired Chief Engineer, even admitted that his part-time teaching job was just a way to escape the tension at home. "At least one of us can be happy this way," he joked. But behind the joke, there was a clear sign of longing for something more.

As the evening continued, the line between contentment and discontent became more pronounced.

The evening eventually wound down, and dinner was more of a formality given how much we'd already eaten. With return gifts from our hosts in hand, we made our way back to the car. As we drove home, the mood shifted to quiet reflection. The cause of happiness and unhappiness, we realized, wasn't our circumstances

- it was us. "Ego and this false sense of superiority will only isolate you. The real joy is in letting go and connecting with others," I mused as we cruised down the highway.

Just then, a cop stopped us, shining his flashlight into the car. "Where are you headed, and what do you do?" he asked. With a cheeky grin, I replied, "We're heading back to our home in Mohali. And with this handlebar moustache, you can probably guess?!"

The cop chuckled, "Army, Jai Hind, Sir. Please go!"

We finally pulled up to our Society at the stroke of midnight. As I parked the car, it hit me - the evening had been more than just a party. It was a reminder. No matter how much wattage we used to carry, the only thing that matters now is the light we bring into each moment, ego-free and full of life.

The story might have ended, but the reflections stayed.

ABBREVIATIONS

AMC - Annual Maintenance Contract
ATR - Action Taken Report
AGBM - Annual General Body Meet
AWHO - Army Welfare Housing Organisation
CME - College of Military Engineering
MD - Managing Director
MES - Military Engineering Service
PD - Project Director
RWA - Residents' Welfare Association
RWS - Residents' Welfare Society
RFID - Radio Frequency Identification
STP - Sewage Treatment Plant
SEPTA - Shivalik Environmental Park and Training Area
TMC - Tenant Management Committee